THE CAMBRIDGE BIBLE COMMENTARY

NEW ENGLISH BIBLE

GENERAL EDITORS

P. R. ACKROYD, A. R. C. LEANEY, J. W. PACKER

THE LETTERS OF PAUL
TO THE EPHESIANS
TO THE COLOSSIANS AND
TO PHILEMON

The Training
Centre

THE CAMBRIDGE BIBLE COMMENTARY

THE LETTERS OF PAUL
TO THE EPHESIANS
TO THE COLOSSIANS AND
TO PHILEMON

COMMENTARY BY

G. H. P. THOMPSON

formerly Vice-Principal of Salisbury Theological College

CAMBRIDGE

AT THE UNIVERSITY PRESS

1967

Published by the Syndics of the Cambridge University Press
Bentley House, 200 Euston Road, London, N.W. 1
American Branch: 32 East 57th Street, New York, N.Y. 10022

Library of Congress Catalogue Card Number: 67-17010

Printed in Great Britain
at the University Printing House, Cambridge
(Brooke Crutchley, University Printer)

GENERAL EDITORS' PREFACE

The aim of this series is to provide the text of the New English Bible closely linked to a commentary in which the results of modern scholarship are made available to the general reader. Teachers and young people preparing for such examinations as the General Certificate of Education at Ordinary or Advanced Level in Britain, and similar qualifications elsewhere, have been especially kept in mind. The commentators have been asked to assume no specialized theological knowledge, and no knowledge of Greek and Hebrew. Bare references to other literature and multiple references to other parts of the Bible have been avoided. Actual quotations have been given as often as possible.

Within these quite severe limits each commentator will attempt to set out the main findings of recent New Testament scholarship, and to describe the historical background to the text. The main theological content of the New Testament will also be critically discussed.

Much attention has been given to the form of the volumes. The aim is to produce books each of which will be read consecutively from first to last page. The introductory material leads naturally into the text, which itself leads into the alternating sections of commentary.

The series is prefaced by a volume—*Understanding the New Testament*—which outlines the larger historical background, says something about the growth and transmission of the text, and answers the question 'Why

should we study the New Testament?' Another volume
—*New Testament Illustrations*—contains maps, diagrams
and photographs.

P. R. A.

A. R. C. L.

J. W. P.

EDITOR'S PREFACE

Although the letter to the Ephesians was written later
than that to the Colossians, the order in which they
appear in the New Testament has been retained here. The
reasons why these letters, with that to Philemon, are
studied together are discussed in a separate note. Within
the limits of a commentary of this length, detailed discussion has not always been possible. But an attempt has
been made to bring out the background against which the
letters were written, to clarify their technical language and
their at times compressed thought, and to show something
of the interest that they hold for us today. My gratitude is
due to all the General Editors for their kindly help and
advice. I am especially indebted to the Reverend J. W.
Packer, who was kind enough to read the whole of my
original draft and make useful comments, and to the
Reverend Dr A. R. C. Leaney, for his thorough and
helpful reading of the final typescript. I should also like to
add my grateful thanks to the Officials of the Cambridge
University Press, who have been so cooperative.

G. H. P. T.

CONTENTS

CONTENTS

PALESTINE

THE SOUTHERN PART OF THE ROMAN
PROVINCE OF ASIA

ix

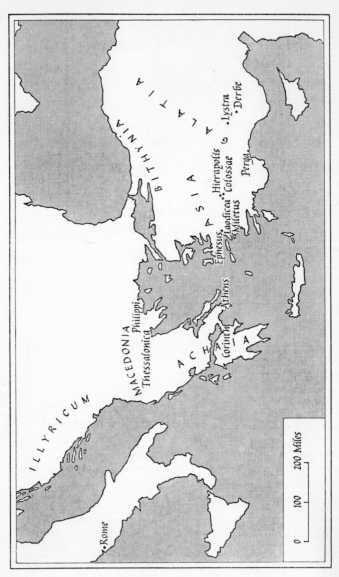

THE MEDITERRANEAN WORLD

x

THREE LETTERS OF
PAUL

✳ ✳ ✳ ✳ ✳ ✳ ✳ ✳ ✳ ✳ ✳ ✳ ✳

WHY WE READ THEM TOGETHER

The letters to the Ephesians, to the Colossians and to Philemon are conveniently taken together for several reasons:

(i) Destination. All three letters were written to churches and people in the Roman Province of Asia (see map, p. ix). The letter to the Colossians was intended for the church at Colossae, and also for the near-by church at Laodicea, to which it was to be passed on (Col. 4: 16, 'And when this letter is read among you, see that it is also read to the congregation at Laodicea, and that you in return read the one from Laodicea'). Similarly, the letter to Philemon, though mainly intended for an individual Christian, is also being sent to Colossae, the home of Philemon, who is the master of the runaway slave Onesimus. The destination of Ephesians is not so clear. In the N.E.B. the opening greeting is: 'From Paul... to God's people at Ephesus'. But, as the N.E.B. footnote makes clear, 'at Ephesus' is omitted in some of the important manuscripts. Marcion (see below, p. 3) seems to have conjectured that Ephesians is the letter, mentioned above, that Paul had written to Laodicea. But this cannot be considered more than a guess. The most likely explanation is that Ephesians was meant to be read in a number of churches in the Province of Asia, of which Ephesus was one.

(ii) Paul in prison. All three letters were written when Paul was undergoing imprisonment (e.g. Eph. 4: 1, 'a prisoner for the Lord's sake'; see also Col. 4: 18, and Philem. 9). They are therefore, with the letter to the Philippians, called 'captivity letters'.

(iii) Tychicus. Colossians and Philemon were clearly written in the same period (see below, p. 114), and Tychicus, Paul's 'dear brother and trustworthy helper', is taking the runaway slave Onesimus and (most likely) the two letters back to Colossae (Col. 4: 7–9). Tychicus is being sent by Paul 'to let you know all about us and to put fresh heart into you'. He is mentioned in a similar way in Eph. 6: 21–22.

(iv) Common Theme. There are close resemblances of language between Ephesians and Colossians, and passages that are parallel to each other. The main subject of each, too, is the unique status and place of Jesus in our efforts to understand the world and its meaning.

The three letters are therefore closely linked together, and throw light on each other.

THE LETTER OF PAUL TO THE EPHESIANS

THE EARLY HISTORY OF THE LETTER

The view is sometimes held that the Revelation of John opens (chapters 2–4) with seven letters to seven churches, because the author already knew of a collection of Paul's letters addressed to the seven centres of Christianity—Rome, Corinth, Galatia, Ephesus, Philippi, Colossae and Thessalonica (see map, p. x). The Revelation was written about A.D. 96, and this evidence would mean that our letter to the Ephesians was known and valued by that date.

The earliest reference to Ephesians seems to be in the letter known as 1 Clement. This was written by Clement, Bishop of

Rome, to the Corinthian Church about A.D. 96. He does not quote directly from Ephesians, but there are indications that he knows it. In 1 Clement 46: 6 the question is asked: 'Or have we not one God, and one Christ, and one Spirit of grace poured out upon us? And is there not one calling in Christ?' This may well be a reminiscence of Eph. 4: 4–6, 'There is one body and one Spirit, as there is also one hope held out in God's call to you; one Lord...one God and Father of all...' Moreover, in 1 Clement 36: 2 and 59: 3 there is the unusual and uncommon phrase 'the eyes of our heart' (i.e. our understanding), which have been 'opened' by the coming of Jesus. This is most easily explained as an echo of Eph. 1: 18, where the N.E.B. translation, 'your inward eyes' is literally, in the original Greek, 'the eyes of your heart'. Such evidence suggests that Ephesians was known and used in the Christian Church by A.D. 96.

In the Christian literature of A.D. 100–150 there are references and allusions to this letter. This literature includes the letters of Bishop Ignatius (A.D. 98–117), the writings of the Shepherd of Hermas (about A.D. 148), and the letter of Bishop Polycarp to the Philippian Church. In the last mentioned letter, written about A.D. 150, Ephesians is quoted as part of the sacred scriptures (12: 1, 'Only, as it is said in these scriptures, "Be ye angry and sin not", and "Let not the sun go down upon your wrath"'). This is a reference to Eph. 4: 26, which the N.E.B. translates: 'If you are angry, do not let anger lead you into sin; do not let sunset find you still nursing it.' By the middle of the second century A.D., the letter quite obviously has a recognized place among the letters of Paul and was regarded as an authoritative writing for the guidance of the Church. For example, between A.D. 140 and 160 Marcion of Sinope made his famous protest against the authority given by the Church to the Old Testament, and to prove his point drew up his own collection of authoritative writings. For this purpose he was able to edit and use a collection of Paul's letters which had been in existence for some time and included Ephesians.

WHO WROTE EPHESIANS?

The opening greeting of the letter would suggest that Ephesians was written, dictated or commissioned by the Apostle Paul himself (1: 1, 'From Paul, apostle of Christ Jesus,...to God's people'). That has been the accepted opinion from the early period of the church onwards until more recent times. For various reasons the theory is often put forward today that Ephesians dates from the period after the death of Paul. On this view the letter is an example of so-called 'pseudonymous' writing (something written by one person under the name of another). Such a method could be used in the ancient world in various circumstances and for different reasons. First, it could be a thorough-going attempt to publish a writing under the name of some authority in order to gain circulation and acceptance for it. Secondly, students were sometimes given the academic exercise of writing, for example, a speech as it might have been composed by some great man of the past. Thirdly, 'pseudonymity' took another turn in some Jewish writings. Here the writer put his message in vivid imagery and in the form of visions which were supposed to have been seen by some great hero of the remote past. The visions are depicted as having been hidden and unknown for many years until the appropriate moment comes. Hence these writings are called 'apocalyptic', i.e. revealing and uncovering God's purpose. An illustration of this is the book of Daniel in the Old Testament, where the hero Daniel is depicted as looking forward over the future course of history. Fourthly, 'pseudonymity' is also thought to have been used as a literary device whereby one wrote in the name of a recognized authority of the past to show: (*a*) that the viewpoint expressed was the kind of approach that that authority would have taken and (*b*) that the writer owed his own understanding of the subject entirely to the other person.

When Ephesians is dated after Paul's death, it is usually considered to be 'pseudonymous' in the fourth sense. We have to imagine a devoted disciple or close associate of Paul following this supposed convention and writing in his master's name. A full discussion is obviously impossible here, but the question has to be asked: Was this literary device, as described above, a recognized tool of the time? We should have to imagine a certain situation arising after the death of Paul, and then someone publishing Ephesians *in Paul's name* to deal with it. Such an idea has been readily accepted, but it would be more convincing if examples were forthcoming from this period of people writing letters or other documents in the name of another with the above motives in view. As far as the present writer knows, such examples are lacking. No true comparison can be drawn between the procedure of the Jewish 'apocalyptic' writers and the procedure that we are considering. In the one case, an ancient figure looks forward over a vast span of history, and sees visions of God's future purposes; in the other, you have a letter written in the name of someone who has died in the recent past and who has been personally known to the 'pseudonymous' writer. Serious reservations must therefore be held about this fourth kind of 'pseudonymity' and doubts expressed whether it was in use in the early church.

WHAT IS MEANT BY AUTHORSHIP?

In the time of Paul there were three senses in which a person could be the author of a letter:

(i) He could 'wield the pen' and actually write the letter for himself.

(ii) He could employ a secretary and dictate the letter. This modern business method was the custom of the time.

(iii) He could give the gist of what he wanted to say to his secretary, and leave the latter to do the composition, which the author could check and correct later. For example, Cicero, a prominent Roman politician of the first century B.C., had letters composed for him in this way by his secretary, Tiro.

Paul normally used method (ii). His letter to the Romans, for instance, was dictated to Tertius (Rom. 16: 22, 'I, Tertius, who took this letter down, add my Christian greetings'). In accordance with the custom of the time the sender would add the final greeting or concluding section in his own handwriting. In copies of ancient letters that have survived, reference is made to a change in the writing at this point. Moreover Cicero, already mentioned, in one of his letters to his brother Quintus, alludes to the fact that he has written the last section in his own handwriting ('When I had written these last words, which are in my own hand, your Cicero came to dinner'). In several of his letters Paul draws special attention to the fact that the final section is in his own handwriting (e.g. Col. 4: 18, 'This greeting is in my hand—PAUL. Remember I am in prison. God's grace be with you'). In Gal. 6: 11, Paul draws attention to the fact that he is now writing himself, and humorously points out that he is using larger letters than his secretary ('You see these big letters? I am now writing to you in my own hand').

Whether Paul ever used method (i) is doubtful, but the possibility of his use of method (iii) must not be ruled out. There may have been circumstances, due to imprisonment or other factors, that forced Paul on occasions to give a fair amount of scope to his secretary or representative.

Against this background is it possible to speak of Paul as the author of Ephesians, or is there something about the letter which demands that it must have been written after his death?

WHAT ARE THE PROBLEMS?

(1) *Language*

The language of Ephesians is akin to that of Paul's other letters, but it also has a large number of new words and phrases which do not occur in such letters as Romans, 1 and 2 Corinthians, Galatians, and 1 Thessalonians, which are normally accepted as Paul's letters belonging to his lifetime. We may take the following examples:

'in the heavenly realms'	(1: 3)
'his Beloved'	(1: 6)
'graciously bestowed'	(1: 6)
'the first to set our hope'	(1: 12)
'community'	(2: 12)
'dividing wall'	(2: 14)
'dwelling'	(2: 22)
'tossed by the waves'	(4: 14)
'devil'	(4: 27)
'potentates'	(6: 12)

The use of new words and phrases can be a very insecure guide in deciding whether a work is written by a particular author. If this method is to be successful, there are two important needs: (*a*) the treatise being examined must be on a larger scale than Ephesians, big enough for some kind of statistical analysis; (*b*) a far larger sample of an author's work is required for comparison than we have in the case of Paul, so that we can judge satisfactorily how wide and rich his vocabulary can be. It is also true that the range of an author's words increases with his widening experience, and that new words may be called for in new situations. For example, the phrase 'tossed by the waves and whirled about by every fresh gust' (4: 14) is not used elsewhere in the Pauline letters, but here it can be said to be demanded by this particular context: the contrast that is being drawn between the stability of the Christian faith and the fickleness of the false theories of life put forward in the contemporary world. Terms may also be taken up from the people against whom one is arguing. In 3: 18, there is reference to 'the breadth and length and height and depth'. The mention of the four dimensions together is found only here in Paul's writings, and may well have been taken over from the language of those who practised magic (the 'deceitful schemes' of 4: 14). Some of the new terms may also be due to the fact that in the circumstances in which Ephesians was written a fair amount of scope was given to Paul's secretary or representative.

A parallel is sometimes seen between the vocabulary of Ephesians and that in works like 1 Clement (already mentioned), the Gospel of Luke, the Acts of the Apostles, 1 Peter and Hebrews, all of which, it is claimed, were written towards the close of the first century A.D. In that case Ephesians ought to be dated to the same period. The relation between Ephesians and these other writings cannot be discussed in detail, but it is important to notice that there is no firm agreement on the dating of these documents. 1 Clement is by common consent placed about A.D. 96, but for the Gospel of Luke and the Acts various dates in the period A.D. 60–100 are often suggested. 1 Peter has been dated as early as A.D. 64–65 or as late as A.D. 111–112, while Hebrews is usually dated about A.D. 75 or even earlier. It must not be ruled out that some of these writers may have known Ephesians (as is almost certainly the case with 1 Clement). Similar language can also be accounted for in different writings by the fact that they may be drawing on a common tradition or source.

The evidence from the language of Ephesians is inconclusive in deciding whether the letter was written after Paul's death.

(2) *Style*

This is thought to be much more cumbersome and involved than Paul's normal livelier style. It has been likened to a 'slowly moving, onwards-advancing mass, like a glacier working its way inch by inch down the valley'. A good illustration of this style can be found in Eph. 1: 3–14. In the Greek text it is one complicated sentence moving slowly and heavily forward; in the N.E.B. translation it is split up into shorter sentences, but something of the original effect can be seen. The same style can be seen very clearly in Eph. 1: 18, 'I pray that your inward eyes may be illumined, so that you may know what is the hope to which he calls you, what the wealth and

glory of the share he offers you among his people in their
heritage, and how vast the resources of his power open to us
who trust in him.'

It is difficult to know just how flexible and varied an author's
style can be unless we possess a larger quantity of his writings
than we do in the case of Paul. The rather cumbersome style
of Ephesians *is* paralleled in other letters of Paul, e.g. Rom. 3:
21–26, which is a single sentence in the Greek, 'But now, quite
independently of law, God's justice has been brought to light.
The Law and the prophets both bear witness to it: it is God's
way of righting wrong, effective through faith in Christ for
all who have such faith—all, without distinction. For all alike
have sinned, and are deprived of the divine splendour, and all
are justified by God's free grace alone, through his act of
liberation in the person of Christ Jesus...' But what is unusual is that in Ephesians this style is sustained without much
relief for long sections. Such a feature may lead us to conclude
that here Paul's secretary or representative has been given
scope in the composition of the letter.

(3) *The Parallels between Ephesians and Colossians*

The striking similarities between the two letters are obvious.
But in some of these parallels, words and phrases are used in
different senses and in different connections. Some examples
are as follows:

(*a*) EPHESIANS	COLOSSIANS
'strangers [Greek: 'alien-ated'] to the community of Israel' (2: 12)	'estranged [Greek: 'alien-ated'] from God' (1: 21)
'For he is himself our peace' (2: 14)	'making peace' (1: 20)
[Jesus] 'has broken down the enmity' (2: 14)	'you were his [God's] ene-mies in heart and mind' (1: 21)

EPHESIANS	COLOSSIANS
'to reconcile the two' (2: 16)	'to reconcile the whole universe' (1: 20) 'God has reconciled you to himself' (1: 22)

In Ephesians the 'alienation' and the 'enmity' are between the Jews and the Gentiles; in Colossians they are between human beings and God. In Ephesians the 'peace' and 'reconciliation' are between Jews and Gentiles; in Colossians they are between God and all his creation.

(b) EPHESIANS 3: 5–6	COLOSSIANS 1: 26–27
'In former generations this [i.e. the secret] was not disclosed; but now it has been revealed that through the Gospel the Gentiles are joint heirs with the Jews.'	'to announce the secret hidden for long ages... The secret is this: Christ in you, the hope of a glory to come.'

In Ephesians God's secret is his plan of uniting Jew and Gentile, which is revealed to the leaders of the Church; in Colossians the secret is Jesus Christ himself and is made known to God's people.

(c) EPHESIANS 3: 2	COLOSSIANS 1: 25
'You have heard how God has assigned the gift of his grace...'	'I became its servant by virtue of the task assigned to me by God'

Here 'assigned the gift' and 'the task assigned' are translations of the same Greek word, which can be rendered as 'stewardship', 'assignment' or 'arrangement'. It is often held (as shown by the N.E.B.) that in the passage from Ephesians the word means 'giving' or 'assigning', while in Colossians it is used in the sense of 'stewardship', i.e. of Paul's office as an apostle. In Eph. 1: 10 and 3: 9, the phrase 'put into effect' is in each case a translation of the same Greek word as above, which now carries the meaning of God's 'arranging' or 'ordering' matters to create harmony in his world. This is a sense of the word not found elsewhere in the letters of Paul.

(d)   EPHESIANS 4: 16   COLOSSIANS 2: 19

'He [Jesus] is the Head, and   'Yet it is from the Head that
on him the whole body   the whole body receives
depends.'   its supplies.'

The view is held that, while in Ephesians the 'body' is the Church, in Colossians the 'body' is the whole universe. The same terms are thought to be used with a different meaning, but this is by no means so clear as in some of the other examples. The 'body' could refer to the Church in each case.

(e)   EPHESIANS 1: 22–23   COLOSSIANS 1: 19

'the church, which...holds   'For in him the complete
within it the fullness'...   being of God...came to
dwell.'

In the above passages 'the fullness' and 'the complete being' are the same word in the Greek. In Ephesians, it is related to the Church; in Colossians it describes Jesus as possessing the 'complete being' of God.

(f)   EPHESIANS 5: 20   COLOSSIANS 3: 17

'in the name of our Lord   'whatever you are doing...
Jesus Christ give thanks...'   do everything in the name
of the Lord Jesus, giving
thanks...'

In Ephesians the clause 'in the name of Jesus' is attached to thanksgiving, while in Colossians it is connected with action.

(g)   EPHESIANS 6: 9   COLOSSIANS 3: 25

'and he has no favourites'   'and he has no favourites'

In Ephesians this appeal to God's lack of favouritism is part of the exhortation to masters, while in Colossians it is addressed to the slaves.

If Paul dictated Ephesians, then he must have done it while the phrases of Colossians (the earlier letter) were still fresh in his memory. In that case would he have used similar language in a different way? This is thought to be unlikely. An easier explanation would be that Ephesians is the work of a follower of Paul who, writing after Paul's death, has reapplied the language of Colossians with which he was very familiar. But it is difficult to weigh up the probabilities: whether such reapplication is more likely to be attributed to Paul himself or to another. If the latter, then it must not be ruled out that he may have been Paul's secretary or representative, who sees how the language of Colossians can be readapted for use in the treatise or letter that Paul has commissioned him to compose. It does seem likely that Paul himself in expressing the ideas contained in Ephesians would by no means have felt so tied to the vocabulary and language of Colossians. On the other hand a person who knew Colossians and who in the same period composed Ephesians for Paul might well have felt a constraint to keep as close as possible to the language of Colossians, and readapt it to put over the message of Ephesians.

(4) *Some unusual features of Ephesians*

These are said to be:

(*a*) The many echoes of impressive passages from other letters of Paul, making Ephesians a 'golden treasury' of Paul's memorable phrases;

(*b*) Passages where a word in the corresponding passage of Colossians seems to have called to mind a passage in another letter and suggested a phrase from the latter context (e.g. the word 'obedient' in Col. 3: 22 has brought to mind Phil. 2: 12, with the result that 'with fear and trembling' has been introduced into the parallel passage of Eph. 6: 5).

It is pointed out that the echoes of Paul's earlier letters in his later ones (e.g. Philippians and Colossians) are on nothing like the same scale as in Ephesians. From (*a*) and (*b*) the conclusion is therefore drawn that Ephesians must be the work of one who has made a thorough reading of Paul's collected letters and absorbed them, and in whose mind memorable passages linger. On the other hand, Ephesians is a general treatise giving a lot of space to God's revelation of himself in Jesus, and its relevance. Therefore the occurrence of Paul's leading theological phrases and terms need not cause surprise. It is worth noting, for instance, that in a passage such as Rom. 5: 1–11, which is full of teaching on leading Christian beliefs, much of the theological terminology of some of the earlier letters is collected. Again, the characteristics mentioned are quite compatible with the idea that Ephesians owes much to Paul's 'secretary' or 'representative', who has lived with Paul, has heard him preach and perhaps dictate his letters, has perhaps seen copies of them and has imbibed his modes of expression.

(5) *Some other supposed difficulties*

(*a*) There was a strong expectation in the early Church that Jesus would come to make his reign fully effective in the near future. This was described as the Advent or Coming of Jesus. An early reference to the belief is found in 1 Thess. 1: 10, 'how you turned from idols, to be servants of the living and true God, and to wait expectantly for the appearance from heaven of his Son Jesus...' In Ephesians there is a lack of emphasis on this 'Advent' teaching. It is not, however, entirely left out, as there appear to be references to it in, e.g. 1: 14 ('when God has redeemed what is his own') and 4: 30 ('...for that Spirit is the seal with which you were marked for the day of our final liberation'). But the main centre of interest is the work and mission of the Church. This might suggest that the letter was written after the death of Paul, when the expectation of the Advent in the near future had faded.

It would, however, be a mistake to think that Paul is dominated by the thought of the Advent. In the letter to the

Galatians, one of Paul's earliest letters, no allusion is made to this doctrine, and later in his ministry he faces the fact that he may die before the Advent takes place (2 Cor. 2: 8, 'We are confident, I repeat, and would rather leave our home in the body and go to live with the Lord'). Very often the emphasis he gives to the Advent depends on the situation being faced. In the second place, there seems to have been a curious tension in the early Church: (i) on the one hand the Advent might come tomorrow; (ii) on the other hand the Church must lead a settled and orderly life in the world, witnessing to what God has done in Jesus Christ and the implications of this. In Ephesians, Paul gives his attention to (ii) because he is discussing, (as we shall see later, p. 22) the Christian contribution to the subject of 'unity' and is showing the *present* security and privileges (as well as responsibilities) of those who belong to the Christian Church.

(*b*) Prominence is given to the 'apostles and prophets' (2: 20; 3: 5), which may point to a time when the leaders of the early Church (including Paul) are dead and venerated as heroes. Would Paul, too, in his lifetime have underlined his own insight into the Gospel, as he does in Eph. 3: 4 ('I have already written a brief account of this, and by reading it you may perceive that I understand the secret of Christ')? But even if the letter is assigned to a time towards the end of the first century A.D., Christian prophets (if not any of the apostles) were certainly still active, and so the problem would still be there. Apart from this, Paul does elsewhere stress the importance of the apostles and the special revelation given to himself (e.g. Gal. 1: 15, 'But then in his good pleasure God who had set me apart from birth and called me through his grace, chose to reveal his Son to me and through me, in order that I might proclaim him among the Gentiles'). The language of Ephesians may seem exaggerated in this respect, but Paul is addressing those who lived in a situation where the leaders of other religions (e.g. the priests of the Mystery cults, for which see pp. 24 and 118 below) laid claim to special understanding, and to special ability to explain the teaching and practices of each particular religion. Paul has to do the same, but off-sets his emphatic claims by an exaggerated statement of his own unworthiness (3: 8). It is hard to imagine a devoted follower of Paul writing in such terms of him after his death.

(c) In Eph. 4: 9–10 it is said that Jesus 'descended to the lowest level, down to the very earth', or better (as in the N.E.B. footnote) 'descended to the regions beneath the earth', a reference to Jesus' death, and his triumph over it. The lack of reference to this 'descent' in Paul's other letters has sug-gested that Ephesians is post-Pauline. But in the popular thought of Paul's day the fear of 'underworld powers' (e.g. the goddesses of fate and the god Pluto) loomed large. These powers were connected with death and disintegration. The Mystery religions (to be discussed below, p. 118) offered security against these powers. Paul, therefore, may well have wished to stress that Jesus himself had successfully and con-clusively invaded the domain of death. The lordship of Jesus over these 'underworld powers' is asserted in the reference to 'the depths' in Phil. 2: 10–11, 'that at the name of Jesus every knee should bow—in heaven, on earth, and in the depths'.

(d) Ephesians has also sometimes been dated later than Paul's lifetime because the Church envisaged by the letter is thought to be composed solely of non-Jews. This was not the state of affairs in the time of Paul. It is true that Ephesians is addressed to Gentiles, but there is nothing to suggest a situa-tion where the Church no longer contains those who had been Jews. On the contrary such a passage as 2: 11 ff. presents Jesus Christ as the meeting-place of Jew and non-Jew (e.g. 2: 14, 'Gentiles and Jews, he has made the two one').

Conclusion

There is nothing in the teaching or views expressed in Ephesians to demand that it should be dated after the death of Paul. Similarly the words and expressions used in the letter are no sure guide in determining the authorship. Due weight has, however, to be given (*a*) to the question of style, (*b*) to the perhaps slavish use of the letter to the Colossians, and (*c*) to the accumulation in this one letter of so many of Paul's memorable expressions. But it would be wrong to draw from this evidence the conclusion that the letter was written later than Paul. The evidence is quite compatible with the idea that the composition of Ephesians owes a great deal to Paul's secretary or representative.

WHY WAS EPHESIANS WRITTEN?

(1) *One Proposed Solution*

Among those who hold that Ephesians was written after the death of Paul, the following theory of its origin has been popular. After the publication of the Acts of the Apostles a new interest arose in the Apostle Paul. An Asian Christian who was well acquainted with the letters to the Colossians and to Philemon had the startling idea that there might be other letters of Paul in existence. A search recovered several of them (Romans, the Corinthian letters, Galatians, Philippians and the letters to Thessalonica) and these together with Colossians and Philemon were published. The letter to the Ephesians was written as a special introduction to the letters, and the 'brief account' mentioned in Eph. 3: 4 refers to the collected letters which were intended to follow ('I have already written a brief account of this, and by reading it you may perceive that I understand the secret of Christ'). The Asian Christian may have been Onesimus the runaway slave, who is the subject of the letter to Philemon.

Starting from the assumption that Ephesians must have been written after Paul's death, this theory gives an interesting account of how and why it came to be written. The basic assumption may, however, be challenged, as we have seen, and the proposed solution itself meets with certain difficulties.

(*a*) It is by no means clear that the 'brief account' mentioned in 3: 4 is a way of referring to a collection of letters that are to follow. It would more naturally be taken to describe an account by Paul of his experience when he was won over to Christianity, when 'God...chose to reveal his Son to me and through me, in order that I might proclaim him among the Gentiles' (Gal. 1: 15).

(b) When a collection of Paul's letters was published, would an introduction to them have been written *in the name of the author*? Moreover, would it have repeated so much of the language and thought of the letters that follow, and given no real indication that it is an introduction to letters? One of the few cases in the ancient world where a collection of writings is prefaced by what we should call a 'Foreword by the Editor' is that of the Jewish book known as Ecclesiasticus or The Wisdom of Jesus, the Son of Sirach. This manual of instruction for carrying out the commandments of God was written about 180 B.C. in the Hebrew language, and was published later in a Greek translation by the author's grandson about 132 B.C. The latter writes a prologue or foreword, which explains the background of the work that follows. It is written not under the name of the author himself, but by the grandson in the first person singular, referring at one stage to 'my grandfather'. Such evidence makes us query the present suggestion about the origin of Ephesians.

(c) The problem also arises why Ephesians lost its place at the head of the letters. From a very early time the letter to the Romans appears first, apparently because it was the longest, and is found in this position in all the early manuscripts. There was also, it seems, another manner of arrangement in the second century A.D., in which the letters to Corinth came first. But there is no evidence that Ephesians ever stood at the head of the collection.

(2) *Another Suggestion*

During Paul's imprisonment at Rome in the period A.D. 59 onwards, problems arose in the churches at Laodicea and Colossae (see map, p. ix). They were faced with the challenge to compromise with other religions (see below, p. 121). This situation led Paul to write the letter to the Colossians, and also a letter to the church at Laodicea (Col. 4: 16) which is now lost. It is accepted here that these letters were written from Rome; for more detailed discussion see below, p. 113. Tychicus, Paul's 'trustworthy helper and fellow servant', was sent on a mission to Asia Minor, which probably included the delivery of the letters. His terms of reference were to 'put fresh heart' into the Christians of Asia Minor (Col. 4: 7–8, 'You will hear all about my affairs from Tychicus, our dear brother and trustworthy helper and fellow-servant in the Lord's work. I am sending him to you on purpose to let you know all about us and to put fresh heart into you').

Tychicus was one of those who accompanied Paul on his journey from Ephesus to Macedonia, and then on the journey to Jerusalem that ended in Paul being taken into safe custody by the Roman authorities (Acts 20–21). Tychicus is called an 'Asian' (Acts 20: 4), i.e. one who came from the Roman province of Asia (see map, p. ix). He was probably a representative of some of the churches which contributed to the collection for the Christian poor at Jerusalem that Paul had been organizing (1 Cor. 16: 1, 'And now about the collection in aid of God's people: you should follow my directions to our congregations in Galatia'). He was apparently in Rome during some stage of Paul's imprisonment described in Acts 28: 16, 30–31. For it is in this period that he is sent on the mission described above. Of the later history of Tychicus we know very little. He is mentioned in Tit. 3: 12, 'When I send Artemas to you, or Tychicus, make haste to join me at Nicopolis'. In 2 Tim. 4: 12, it is said that he has been sent to Ephesus. If the letters to Timothy and the letter to Titus belong to the closing years of Paul's ministry, or contain reminiscences of that period, then these passages show that Tychicus continued to be an important helper of Paul.

On his present mission to Colossae, Tychicus would be at a distance from Rome and so would have to be given a certain amount of scope to take whatever measures seemed necessary. Paul may well have commissioned Tychicus to issue further messages to the Churches of Asia Minor under the Apostle's name, and may have told him the sort of line that he ought to take.

After his arrival in Asia Minor, Tychicus saw the need for a general 'manifesto' to be read to the Christian congregations of that area to show how the Christian faith could meet the aspirations and fears facing people of that time, and to remind Christians of their responsibilities and privileges. That 'manifesto' is our present Ephesians, composed by Tychicus, but presenting the Gospel in the phraseology, language and ideas used by Paul, with which Tychicus was thoroughly familiar; he was naturally influenced by the letter to the Colossians, which had been written to deal with similar problems. As it was to be read to different congregations in Asia Minor, Tychicus or the elder reading it would fill in the name of the church in the opening sentence. Ephesus was one (but only one) of these churches; hence in some of the manuscripts this name is included in 1:1 and in others omitted. Another possibility is that 'Ephesus' was inserted later because it was one of the big centres of Paul's missionary activity (Acts 19). Naturally, as in Col. 4:7, so in Eph. 6:21, there is reference to Tychicus and the authority delegated to him by Paul. As Ephesians is a general manifesto written in Asia by Tychicus, this may be why it differs from Colossians in having no concluding greetings from people with Paul, though it is worth noting that the letter to the Galatians also has no such greetings.

Ephesians may therefore be regarded as a manifesto giving hope and encouragement to Christians in Asia Minor. It shows the benefits that the Christian faith has to offer to all men, the place of the Church in God's purposes, and what is involved in living the Christian life. In the course of this discussion it also deals with questions that were of current interest in the time of Paul and gives the Christian contribution to their solution. These questions are in one way or another connected with the theme of 'unity' and to this subject we now turn.

THE CONTEMPORARY INTEREST IN 'UNITY'— THE CHRISTIAN CONTRIBUTION

Unity as a 'Talking-Point' in the First Century A.D.

In this period the theme of 'unity' was in different ways very much to the fore and was occupying people's minds and attention. We may take some examples of this.

The interest in 'unity' was shown for instance by the Stoics with whom Paul came into contact in Athens (Acts 17: 18, 'And some of the Epicurean and Stoic philosophers joined issue with him'). They were a school of philosophy founded by Zeno of Cyprus (350–250 B.C.), and took their name from the painted *stoa* or portico in which Zeno used to teach. The Stoics saw an order and design in the universe which gave it an underlying unity. There were two basic principles in the world, one passive and one active. The passive substance is matter, and is the stuff out of which everything is made. The other, the active principle, is the reason, which is in and through everything and by which everything is as it is. The basis of all life in this world is heat, which gives growth, vitality and life; this heat is not, however, destructive, but gives everything its life and health and in the case of man his intelligence. Part of the Stoic *Hymn of Cleanthes* may be quoted, where this 'reason' is being praised:

> 'But skill to make the crooked straight is thine,
> To turn disorder into fair design;
> Ungracious things are gracious in thy sight,
> For ill and good thy power doth so combine
> That out of all appears in unity
> Eternal Reason,...'

Unity was also in men's minds because the Roman imperial system under the first emperor, Augustus, and his successors had brought unification of a large area of the Mediterranean world, helped by improved communications. Those who possessed Roman citizenship, like Paul himself (e.g. Acts 16: 37), must have had the sense of belonging to a far larger whole. The Stoics believed that the world was one big city, to which all belonged. Some of them were known to say: 'I am a citizen of the world.' They sometimes held a vision of a world-wide commonwealth, in which all would have equal status.

This sense of 'unity' or 'growing together' was also seen in that other feature of the times—the belief that all religions are at root the same. The result was that the different religious cults took over ideas from each other. Such was the case with the Mystery religions—a prominent and flourishing movement at this time (see below, p. 118)—which were also feeling after 'unity' of another kind. There was a desire to come to terms with life. This meant in the first place the attempt to escape the various powers and forces that made human existence fearful and unbearable. In the second place it involved being at one with gods that could guarantee such an escape. This might be called the search for 'harmony'. Such a deliverance was thought to be attained through union with the god of the particular cult (e.g. Isis or Serapis), and was helped forward by the feeling of being at one with fellow human beings in the fellowship of common meals.

There was also the quest for the attainment of 'unity' in the individual self, and freedom from the tensions that upset and split the personality. How was one to attain what modern psychologists would call 'integration of the self'? Both the Stoics (already mentioned), and another sect of philosophy, the Epicureans, had a recipe to offer to attain this end. For the Stoic, 'fate' was an important word. This fate was not a blind, helpless sequence of events, but the active and wise power that regulates the world. If a person wants to find happiness and peace, he must assent to whatever happens, in the certainty that it comes from the will of this kindly fate, and so must be good. In other words, the Stoics taught: If you cannot get what you want, teach yourself to want what you get! This should be possible for you to accept, because you know that everything comes from God, and so must be good. In this way a man is freed from tension, and achieves balance. The Epicureans were a school of philosophy founded by Epicurus (341–270 B.C.). The aim of Epicurus' teaching was to help people to attain a state of tranquillity. The great enemy of tranquillity is fear and particularly the fear of death and the fear of the gods. Epicurus tried to show that these fears were ill founded, and that their removal would lead to calm content and self-sufficiency.

In all these various ways people of Paul's time were looking for 'unity'.

THE CONTRIBUTION OF EPHESIANS

The letter has something to say of relevance to this search for different kinds of 'unity'.

(1) *What makes the world one*

From the Christian viewpoint the world finds its underlying unity in 'the one God and Father of all, who is over all and through all and in all' (4: 6)—a *personal* God, not just a principle. Belief in such a unity is not, however, a matter of speculation, but has received a demonstration in a historical character, Jesus Christ, who is God's Son (1: 3) and stands in a unique relationship to him. He is 'Saviour' (5: 23) because through his life, death and resurrection he has brought the assurance of God's love and favour (1: 6–8; 2: 4, 'But God, rich in mercy, for the great love he bore us, brought us to life...') and made access to him possible (2: 18; 3: 12, 'In him we have access to God with freedom'). Hence the best description of God is 'Father' (1: 2; 2: 18; 3: 14). God has here given his sign that he will be *the* sovereign in his world over all that opposes him (1: 20, '...when he enthroned him at his right hand in the heavenly realms'). Jesus has triumphed over the forces that tried to oppose him and reduce him to nothingness; he is enthroned as King (1: 20; 4: 8) and Lord (4: 5) with claims on human allegiance. Jesus Christ is therefore the focal point where all and everything in the world are to find their meeting-point with God (1: 10, 'namely that the universe, all in heaven and on earth, might be brought into a unity in Christ'). In other words, in asking the 'why and the wherefore' of the world and human existence, one starts with Jesus Christ.

(2) *A citizenship of all human beings*

In the church, the society founded by Jesus, people of all races, classes and nationalities can find a citizenship (2: 19, 'Thus you are no longer aliens in a foreign land, but fellow-citizens with God's people'). While God was preparing for the coming of Jesus Christ, he made use of a limited citizenship (like the Roman kind), which only Jews possessed (2: 11–12, '...you were at that time...strangers to the community of Israel'), and the basis of this citizenship was the Old Testament Law (2: 15, '...the law with its rules and regulations'). But this was only a temporary arrangement 'until the time was ripe' (1: 10), and through the work of Jesus Christ the citizenship was opened up to all and the barrier between Jew and non-Jew broken down (2: 14). God has now made a new 'covenant' or arrangement, which includes all men (2: 13, 'you who once were far off have been brought near through the shedding of Christ's blood').

(3) *Where all religions meet*

Ephesians answers the 'all religions are the same' attitude *not* by saying that the leading features of all religions should be combined. It issues the more drastic challenge that Christianity gives *the* answer to the search of all religions and so is *the* cult to end all cults. This is implied in 4: 4 ('There is one body', i.e. 'one religious society') and 4: 14 (the warning against other solutions to the problems of life). Some characteristics of this Christian society may be noted:

(*a*) *The Christian secret.* Secrecy marked the ceremonies and the knowledge offered by the Mystery religions (see below, p. 118); but for Christians the only 'secret' or 'hidden purpose' (1: 9; 3: 4; 3: 9) is an *open* secret—God's plan of reconciling everything to himself in Jesus Christ. It was kept 'hidden', but only until the right moment. In the Mystery cults the important thing was to be initiated into the secrets of the particular cult, and to undergo certain mysterious rites. This was the way to security. At the head of these cults there were priests and prophets who were sometimes called 'mystagogues', because they introduced people to the secrets and mysteries of the cult and claimed to have special powers for this task. Similarly the Church has her apostles and prophets who can explain God's purposes openly (3: 5, 'but now it has been revealed by inspiration to his dedicated apostles and prophets').

(*b*) *The function of the Church.* The Church exists to witness to Jesus Christ, the starting-point for the understanding of human life, and to hold fast to the full implications of it (4: 3, 'Spare no effort to make fast with bonds of peace the unity which the Spirit gives'). The leaders of the Church are there to equip it for this work (4: 12). The Christian fellowship can also be described as an organism owing its life to Jesus Christ, its 'head', and thriving on 'love' (4: 16). It can also be likened to a building (2: 20) which is to take the form of a temple, i.e. a centre where God is acknowledged and met with. It will therefore also be a centre of light, reflecting God's will (5: 7), and showing up what is contrary to it (5: 11, 'take no part in the barren deeds of darkness but show them up for what they are').

(*c*) *Enlightenment.* The followers of the Mystery cults sometimes went through various stages of enlightenment. This might involve the use of holy water and various kinds of herbs. The Christian life is to be an advance in understanding (i) the great privileges and assurance that follow from being reconciled to God (1: 18–19) and (ii) the full extent of the self-giving love shown by Jesus Christ (3: 17–18, '...may you be strong to grasp, with all God's people, what is the breadth and length and height and depth of the love of Christ, and to know it'). It is being drawn by this love that brings poise and balance and 'fullness of being' for which men are looking (3: 19). This kind of love is the mark of the full Christian life, and Christians have to face its implications for everyday living. Some of these implications are given in 4: 25 — 5: 5 (pieces of practical advice) and in 5: 22 — 6: 9 (advice on family and social relationships). Therefore, to know God's 'secret' is not a way of escaping from life in this world but of understanding how this present life is to be lived.

(*d*) *The conflict with evil.* The theme of the struggle of man with evil is prominent in many religions, sometimes symbolized as a conflict between light and darkness. In Paul's day, the cult of Mithra, which originated in Persia, was very much concerned with the struggle between light and darkness. Mithra himself was thought of as the god of light, who, it was claimed, could help suffering man. A similar conflict was familiar to Jewish thought. For example, the Jewish sect at Qumran, of which we have learnt a great deal from the Dead Sea Scrolls, saw themselves as the 'sons of light' engaged in a conflict with darkness, i.e. the forces of evil (see *The Dead Sea Scrolls in English*, G. Vermes, Penguin Books, 1962). In Ephesians, Paul stresses that God, the creator of the world, has had a showdown with the forces opposed to him, and therefore Christians, because they have taken their stand at God's side, must be involved in the same struggle with evil (6: 10–20). But in this struggle there are the armour and weapons provided by the victorious mission of Jesus Christ (6: 10, 'Finally then, find your strength in the Lord, in his mighty power').

(*e*) *The Church's joyful enthusiasm.* In some of the Mystery religions, liquors and drinks of various kinds were employed to induce ecstasy and excitement; hence, perhaps, Paul's attack on drunkenness (5: 18), and his point that Christians are to be 'drunk', but with a joy that comes from 'thanksgiving'. Similarly the Mysteries were celebrated with noisy songs and clashing of instruments, which could develop into pure frenzy. Paul says that songs, hymns and psalms play an important part in the Church's public worship and fellowship, but these are only the outward expression of gratitude to God for all his mercies (5: 19).

(4) *The union with the 'One Lord'*

The other cults had their 'Lords'. For example Serapis, the god of a religious cult which started in Egypt, was called 'Lord', and similarly the cry 'The Emperor is Lord' was used in the worship of the Roman Emperor. But, as Jesus Christ is the point where the world finds its unity, he is the 'One Lord' that matters (4: 5), the 'supreme head' of the Church (1: 22). But whereas the Mystery religions often based their knowledge of their gods on legends and fairy tales, the 'Lord' Jesus is known through having lived and died as a historical character (e.g. 5: 2, 'and live in love as Christ loved you, and gave himself up on your behalf').

Union with the lord of the cult was important for all these religions. Union with Jesus Christ is sometimes described by the phrase 'in Christ' (1: 3). This conjures up the picture of Jesus Christ as an organism of which Christians form the living parts. Such close unity with Jesus Christ is gained by 'faith' or personal allegiance to him and all that he stands for (2: 8; 4: 5). The importance attached to personal loyalty to the Lord distinguishes Christianity from the other Mystery religions. This 'faith' is outwardly expressed and dramatized in the rite of 'baptism' or immersion in water (see on 4: 23-24; 5: 26), which rivals the ceremonies of the Mystery religions. Such a union may also be described as a 'sacred marriage' between Jesus Christ and his Church (see on 5: 25-33). The idea was not unknown to the Mysteries, though it was sometimes depicted in very crude ceremonies.

The result of this union with Jesus Christ is:

(a) 'resurrection' or 'enthronement' with Jesus (2: 6), i.e. sharing his triumph over all the forces that tried to break him.

(b) 'rebirth' (another benefit offered by the other religions). This involves the throwing off of one's old self-centred character, and the 'taking over' of the character seen in the human life of Jesus Christ as that into which one has to grow (4: 22–24). Thus the qualities of character seen in a *historical* person are of vital importance for Christians (again a contrast with the Mystery cults).

(c) the experience of the Holy Spirit of God, the one source of 'drive' for living the God-centred life (3: 16; 4: 5). This God-given help here and now is the pledge of his favour and of future blessings (1: 14, 'and that Spirit is the pledge that we shall enter upon our heritage'). It may therefore be described as the 'seal' or 'guarantee', assuring the Christian of God's love (4: 30, 'for that Spirit is the seal with which you were marked for the day of our final liberation'), just as the followers of other cults were sealed or branded with a mark on their foreheads.

(5) *The life of 'harmony'*

Such harmony or 'freedom' (3: 12) is secured by being right with the God who 'created everything' (3: 10). It is made possible through the work of Jesus Christ. This being at one with God can be called 'salvation' or 'deliverance' (1: 13; 6: 17), and brings the privilege of being adopted as sons of a personal God (1: 5, 'and he destined us—such was his will and pleasure—to be accepted as his sons'). Such a status is no cause for pride, as it is based on God's will and purpose (1: 4, 8), on his call (4: 4) and his freely shown favour (1: 6; 2: 8). But a jarring discord in life is also caused by a feeling of guilt and failure to live up to what is right. In Jesus Christ and particularly through his death on the cross (1: 7) God's forgivingness is brought home to men; 'the resources of his power open to us' are also underlined (1: 19; 3: 20; 6: 10).

'Hope' too is a feature of the 'life of harmony'. It was an attraction of the Mystery cults, which often held out the rosy prospect of a happy immortality after death. The theme of 'hope' is prominent in Ephesians (4: 4, 'one hope held out in God's call to you'). God will work out his plan, and Christians will have a place in that plan (1: 14). This will mean 'liberation' in the sense of enjoying full fellowship with God (4: 30). The letter ends with a prayer that those 'who love the Lord Jesus Christ' may attain 'immortality' of this kind. No extravagant prospects are outlined for Christians after death. The implication is that the Christian goes into the future with a firm conviction of God's love and protection. That is sufficient.

✻　✻　✻　✻　✻　✻　✻　✻　✻　✻　✻　✻　✻

The Glory of Christ in the Church

GREETING

1 FROM PAUL, apostle of Christ Jesus, commissioned by the will of God, to God's people at Ephesus, believers incorporate in Christ Jesus.

2 Grace to you and peace from God our Father and the Lord Jesus Christ.

✼ The opening greeting follows the pattern of that of other letters of the time. These usually began: 'So-and-so to so-and-so greeting' (e.g. Acts 23: 26, which translated literally is: 'Claudius Lysias to His Excellency the Governor Felix greeting'). Paul expands this by giving details of his status and that of those addressed. He also extends the usual term 'greeting' into *Grace to you and peace*.

Grace in the Greek has the same ring about it as the Greek word for 'greeting'.

peace may have been suggested by the common Jewish greeting 'Peace be with you'.

1. *apostle* means an ambassador or representative with full powers. The qualifications for the position of apostle are not exactly known, but the apostles formed the highest rank of ministers in the early church (e.g. 1 Cor. 12: 28, 'Within our community God has appointed, in the first place apostles ...'). The term originally applied to 'the Twelve' (e.g. Luke 6: 13, 'he [Jesus] called his disciples to him, and from among them he chose twelve and named them Apostles'). It was then extended to include Paul and others who had a special commission from God. An important function of the apostles was that of preaching the gospel (1 Cor. 1: 17, 'Christ did not send me to baptize, but to proclaim the Gospel'). They also had the special task of founding and supervising communities of Christians (1 Cor. 9: 2, 'for you are yourselves the very seal of my apostolate'). Paul traced his own calling as an apostle to the vision of the Risen Jesus that he had on the Damascus Road (Acts 9; Gal. 1: 15, 'But then in his good pleasure God, who had set me apart from birth and called me through his grace, chose to reveal his Son to me and through me, in order that I might proclaim him among the Gentiles'). Hence Paul's reference here to being *commissioned by the will of God*. Though sure of his call to be an apostle, Paul always felt his own unworthiness for the position (see 3: 8 below and especially 1 Cor. 15: 8–9, 'In the end he [Jesus] appeared even to me; though this birth of mine was monstrous, for I had persecuted the church of God and am therefore inferior to all other apostles—indeed not fit to be called an apostle').

God's people (Greek: 'those set apart by God') was used to describe the Jewish nation, through whom God prepared for the coming of Jesus. It now describes the followers of Jesus, as those who are put right with God and are committed to serving him.

at Ephesus is omitted in some manuscripts, but the text would be incomplete without a place name. The suggestion has already been made that Ephesians is a manifesto to be read in the churches of Asia Minor. Usually, with a circular letter of this kind, there would be a general reference, in the opening greeting, to those who were being addressed (e.g. Gal. 1: 2, 'I and the group of friends now with me send greetings to the Christian congregations of Galatia'). In the present case it is possible to imagine that, when Ephesians was read out to each local congregation of Christians, the appropriate name would be inserted by Tychicus or those responsible for presenting the letter. Ephesus was probably one of the churches concerned (see map, p. ix).

believers is almost a technical term for Christians who stake their all on Jesus.

incorporate: Jesus is seen as an organism to which Christians belong as parts; it is only this sense of so belonging that gives them confidence.

2. This is no vague wish; it is a prayer that God's *grace* (his loving favour) and his *peace* (his hand of friendship) may be the most important things in the lives of these Christians. Both are made available in the mission of Jesus.

our Father. The term speaks of God's accessibility and loving responsibility for his creation; it is the work of the *Lord Jesus Christ* that brings home to us these qualities of God. Jesus taught his followers to address God as 'Our Father' (Matt. 6: 9). See also below on verse 3.

the Lord is a title of the Risen and Exalted Jesus. It suggests the triumph of Jesus over all the forces that tried to reduce him to nothing, and describes him as the one in whom God confronts us with his claim to be King. In the Old Testament 'Lord' is one of the names of God, and in the world contemporary with Paul was used of the gods of the various religious cults (e.g. 1 Cor. 8: 5, 'as indeed there are many "gods" and many "lords" '). The title therefore describes the divine status of Jesus, and also stresses the loyalty that is demanded of those who acknowledge that 'Jesus is Lord'. The latter is one of the earliest ways in which faith in Jesus was openly confessed by the candidate at his baptism, and by the Christian congregation at worship (Rom. 10: 9, 'If on your lips is the confession, "Jesus is Lord", and in your heart the faith that God raised him from the dead, then you will find salvation').

Jesus was a fairly common Jewish name—the equivalent of Joshua. It was given at circumcision (Luke 2: 21, 'Eight days later the time came to circumcise him, and he was given the name Jesus'). 'Jesus' is closely connected with a Hebrew word meaning 'to save', and in the case of Jesus of Nazareth was seen to be significant (Matt. 1: 21, 'and you shall give him the name Jesus (Saviour), for he will save his people from their sins').

Christ was at first a title describing Jesus as 'the Christ' or 'the Messiah', 'the Anointed One', i.e. the King who would come to deliver the Jews from their enemies and give them security. The early disciples of Jesus claimed that he was this expected king, but not in the sense of being an earthly king or of setting up an earthly kingdom. We may note Peter's challenge in Acts 2: 36 ('Let all Israel then accept as certain that God has made this Jesus, whom you crucified, both Lord and Messiah'). As this title did not convey very much to those who had not been brought up in the Jewish faith, it soon became part of the name of Jesus, as here.

This full title *the Lord Jesus Christ* therefore brings out the important fact that there is an identity of person between the Risen Jesus, who is the centre of the Church's loyalty here and now, and the historical Jesus of Nazareth, who lived at a particular time on earth and was crucified by order of Pontius Pilate, the Roman Governor of Judaea (A.D. 26–36).

When we read of Jesus of Nazareth in the Gospels (e.g. of his love), we know what the Risen Jesus is like here and now. *

CHRISTIAN SONSHIP

3 Praise be to the God and Father of our Lord Jesus Christ, who has bestowed on us in Christ every spiritual blessing
4 in the heavenly realms. In Christ he chose us before the world was founded, to be dedicated, to be without
5 blemish in his sight, to be full of love; and he destined us—such was his will and pleasure—to be accepted as his
6 sons through Jesus Christ, that the glory of his gracious gift, so graciously bestowed on us in his Beloved, might redound to his praise.

* Paul often, as here, begins his letters with an act of praise or thanksgiving to God. 1: 3-14 is a single sentence in the Greek, but in the N.E.B. has been divided for clarity into a number of separate sentences. The phrase 'in Christ' keeps recurring. This is Paul's way of underlining the importance of Jesus for the understanding of God and his purposes.

3. *Praise be to God* was the usual Jewish phrase for acknowledging the greatness of God. But Christians have to add *Father of our Lord Jesus Christ* because in Jesus God has been encountered much more closely.

Father here describes the special and unique relationship between God and Jesus. Jesus in his earthly life dared to address God with the very intimate term 'Abba' (Mark 14: 36, 'Abba, Father,' he said, 'all things are possible to thee'). 'Abba' is rather like 'daddy' or 'papa', or other endearing terms that people use to show their affection and closeness to others. The right of Jesus to make this claim was justified when Jesus appeared to his disciples alive from the dead, and so demonstrated decisively to them that death by crucifixion had not put an end to him and his claims. In turn the early Christians felt that Jesus had given them the assurance to address God in the same intimate way (Gal. 4: 6, 'To prove that you are sons, God has sent into our hearts the Spirit of his Son, crying "Abba! Father!"'). See also above on verse 2.

blessing: a benefit given to human beings by God. The blessing is *spiritual* either because it is given by God or because it is not a material one, but consists in being reconciled to God.

in the heavenly realms can mean that the benefit is guaranteed by God or that it brings the privilege of sharing in the life of God *in Christ*, i.e. through being linked with him.

4. When the early Christians said that God *chose* them before the foundation of the world, they expressed their conviction that: (*a*) they owed their new status with God to his loving care and (*b*) they had an important part to play in God's purposes for the world. This did not prevent them from also saying that they had made a personal choice of Jesus as their Lord (e.g. 1: 13, 'when you had heard the message...and had believed it').

dedicated: God's choice is not sheer privilege, but brings with it the responsibility of being fully committed to his cause.

without blemish was used by the Jews to describe the perfect condition required in the animal offered in sacrifice to God. Here it describes the perfect obedience to God that is required of Christians. This obedience is expressed in a self-giving *love* to others.

5. It is possible that (as in the N.E.B. footnote) verse 4 should end at *sight*. In that case our present verse will begin: 'In his love he destined us'. The reference will then be to God's own generously given love.

destined, *will* and *pleasure* all stress that to be right with God is not attained by human merit, but is something due to his sheer goodness.

accepted: literally 'adopted'. Adoption of someone into a

family was common Roman practice. Through his obedience Jesus showed himself the true Son of God. He thus bridges the gap between us and God and assures us of entrance into God's family with the dignified status of sons (Gal. 4: 4–5, 'God sent his own Son, born of a woman, born under the law...in order that we might attain the status of sons').

6. God's *glory*, i.e. his splendour and greatness, is seen in his coming down to our level in Jesus, an act which is a *gracious gift* and *graciously bestowed* because it is the result of God's freely given love, and is not earned or merited by human beings.

his Beloved was used in the Old Testament to describe the nation Israel and the special part that it had to play in God's revealing of himself (e.g. Isa. 5: 1, 'Let me sing for my well-beloved a song of my beloved touching his vineyard'). It now describes Jesus as the one specially chosen to make God better known. Christians are, as it were, living 'showrooms', displaying God's *gracious gift*, i.e. his offer of friendship in Jesus Christ; they are therefore centres of *praise*. A good illustration of this verse is found in the saying of Jesus in Matt. 5: 16, 'And you, like the lamp, must shed light among your fellows, so that, when they see the good you do, they may give praise to your Father in heaven.' *

GOD UNFOLDS HIS PURPOSE

7 For in Christ our release is secured and our sins are forgiven through the shedding of his blood. Therein lies the
8 richness of God's free grace lavished upon us, imparting
9 full wisdom and insight. He has made known to us his hidden purpose—such was his will and pleasure deter-
10 mined beforehand in Christ—to be put into effect when the time was ripe: namely, that the universe, all in heaven and on earth, might be brought into a unity in Christ.

✻ Where is an underlying purpose to be found to make sense of the universe and of human life? Paul claims that this purpose is uncovered in Jesus.

7. *release*, a word used of the freeing of slaves from bondage. People are free when they do the will of God and so carry out the purpose for which they were made. *Sins* are not just the breaking of a law, but are acts of disloyalty to a personal God. They are a sign of human slavery.

through the shedding of his blood, i.e. Jesus' death on the cross. The Jews believed that the blood in animals was their life (Deut. 12: 23, 'for the blood is the life'). When, therefore, animals were sacrificed to God and their blood released, a new and living relationship with God was created. For example, this was the way in which the covenant or agreement between God and the Jews had originally been made (e.g. Exod. 24: 8, 'And Moses took the blood and sprinkled it on the people, and said, Behold the blood of the covenant, which the Lord hath made with you concerning all these words'). Jesus was convinced that through his death a new and closer relationship between God and man would be established (1 Cor. 11: 25, 'In the same way he (Jesus) took the cup after supper, and said: "This cup is the new covenant sealed by my blood"'). The shedding of Jesus' *blood* is also the outward sign of his willingness to give himself to the uttermost for human beings. Further, because of his own unique relationship to God, his self-givingness is a revealing of the depths of God's love and brings with it the assurance that *our sins are forgiven*, i.e. the slate of the past is wiped clean, and we are given a new start. In all this there is demonstrated *the richness of God's free grace*, i.e. his love and kindness shown without thought of human merit or desert. In this way Paul often stresses that our relationship with God is not a reward for what we have done, but a response to God's prior love.

8. The following verse shows what the *wisdom* and *insight* are.

9. *hidden purpose* (Greek: 'mystery') means something that

has been hidden or secret but which God at the right moment has made known.

Determined beforehand stresses God's readiness and power to do what the situation demands.

10. *The time was ripe* for the coming of Jesus in several senses. The Jewish nation had been taken into confidence by God; they had been brought to see that the world was one, created by *one* God, who was righteous and demanded righteousness, and who would at the right moment act to reveal himself to the whole world. Jewish thought and understanding of God forms the background to the mission of Jesus. The time was ripe also because the Roman Empire had brought the so-called Roman Peace and settled road communications, which helped the missionary work of Paul and others. There was also a general feeling towards a way of life that could give a sense of security.

The last part of the verse recognizes that a disunity has crept into God's world. *heaven* is here a way of describing the invisible part of the universe, and *all in heaven* describes superhuman forces of evil at work against God. These malignant powers are trying to rival God and keep him from his proper place.

On earth there are divisions among people and nations, and also human disobedience to God's will. In Jesus God has provided a 'meeting-point' where the forces at work against him are challenged and the world summoned to find a new unity. ✻

CHRISTIAN PRIVILEGES

11 In Christ indeed we have been given our share in the heritage, as was decreed in his design whose purpose is
12 everywhere at work. For it was his will that we, who were the first to set our hope on Christ, should cause his
13 glory to be praised. And you too, when you had heard the message of the truth, the good news of your salvation,

and had believed it, became incorporate in Christ and received the seal of the promised Holy Spirit; and that 14 Spirit is the pledge that we shall enter upon our heritage, when God has redeemed what is his own, to his praise and glory.

* The blessings of Christians are now mentioned, but they are not a cause for pride, as it is God's 'praise' and 'glory' that matter. This point is stressed in both verses 12 and 14.

11. *we* is sometimes taken to refer to Jewish Christians in contrast to *you* (i.e. gentile Christians) in verse 13. More probably *we* includes all Christians of whom the *you* form a part. The *heritage* is the Christians' new status of being right with God. This status is secure because it is based on the *purpose* of God, who not only plans, but can carry out what he plans. Paul has a firm faith in the power of God (see also 3: 7 and 3: 20–21).

12. As it stands, this verse describes Jewish Christians, who were the first to accept the Gospel. There is another possible translation given in the N.E.B. footnote, and this is preferable: 'we, whose expectation and hope are in Christ'. Christians have staked their all on the fact that Jesus offers the key to life. Therefore they are a kind of 'display centre' advertising, for all to see, the claims of God on his world; they are in this way to 'cause his glory to be praised'.

13. Paul reminds those addressed that they belong to the *we* of the previous verses. The *truth* is the true understanding of what God is like (see also John 1: 17, 'Grace and truth came through Jesus Christ').

salvation is being rescued from wrong ideas of human life and being put in touch with the God who matters; it is this kind of safety that Jesus brings, and so it can be described as *good news*. This language is used in the Old Testament of God coming to rescue his people (e.g. Isa. 52: 7, 'How beautiful upon the mountains, are the feet of him that bringeth good tidings, that publisheth peace...that publisheth salvation; that saith unto Zion, Thy God reigneth!').

believed means not only accepting the *good news* as a fact, but staking one's whole life upon it. This belief was publicly demonstrated in baptism, through which those addressed became *incorporate in Christ*, i.e. part of him, like the parts of a living organism. But just as the part shares in the life of the organism, so to belong to Jesus Christ means to share in God's living power, his *Spirit*. The Holy Spirit was the phrase which the Jews used to describe the creative power of God (Ezek. 36: 27, 'And I will put my spirit within you, and cause you to walk in my statutes'). The work of Jesus brought about a greater opportunity for the working of this power in the world.

promised probably refers to Jesus' promise of the Holy Spirit to his disciples (e.g. Luke 24:49, 'And mark this: I am sending upon you my Father's promised gift'). The signature and *seal* on an agreement guarantee its binding force; the experience of God's Holy Spirit in the lives of Christians is the guarantee of God's favour. (For the importance of the Holy Spirit for the early Church, see also below, p. 65.)

the pledge is a term taken from what in the ancient world might be called the equivalent of our hire-purchase or credit system. It is the deposit or down payment paid to secure an article and the guarantee of the ultimate possession of the article, if the further payments due are completed.

heritage means a place in God's final kingdom, when God has fully reclaimed his world.

to his praise and glory, i.e. God will finally be the only centre of worship. ✳

CHRISTIAN INSIGHT

15 Because of all this, now that I have heard of the faith you have in the Lord Jesus and of the love you bear
16 towards all God's people, I never cease to give thanks

for you when I mention you in my prayers. I pray that 17
the God of our Lord Jesus Christ, the all-glorious Father,
may give you the spiritual powers of wisdom and vision,
by which there comes the knowledge of him. I pray that 18
your inward eyes may be illumined, so that you may
know what is the hope to which he calls you, what the
wealth and glory of the share he offers you among his
people in their heritage, and how vast the resources of 19
his power open to us who trust in him.

✱ Paul knows that the Christian life can never be one of
'standstill'. It must be a growth in wonder at the privileges
which God has given and a growth in full understanding of
all their implications. Hence Paul's prayer in this present
passage.

1: 15–23 is again one long sentence in the Greek which
the N.E.B. translation has divided into shorter sentences.

15. *I have heard* implies that Paul himself has not met the
Christians addressed, or at least has not seen them recently.
faith is loyalty or allegiance to Jesus and all that he stands for,
and so involves the showing of loving care for the welfare of
others, here other Christians. There is something lacking, for
example, in a Christian congregation that is wrapped up in its
own needs and pays no attention to the needs of other Christians in other parts of the world.

16. Thanksgiving to God serves as a constant reminder of
all that we owe to God and his goodness (compare Phil. 1: 3,
'I thank my God whenever I think of you').

17. The God to whom Paul prays is not remote and unknown, but revealed in a historical figure, Jesus. God can
therefore be called *Father*, which tells us that he is accessible to
us and has a loving responsibility for us. But he is also *all-glorious*, to be regarded with awe and wonder as the source of
all being and life. *spiritual powers* should not suggest that God
uses some kind of extra sense to make himself known. He

uses the human mind and human experience, which he stimulates in various ways, sometimes through the challenge of certain historical events. For example it was the early disciples' experience of Jesus in his life and after his death that made them conclude that he was the all-decisive figure in God's dealings with men. The Christian never stands 'still, but should be growing in *knowledge* of God, i.e. insight into the full implications of what God has done in Jesus.

Paul's prayer here makes us think of the purpose and nature of prayer in the thought of Jesus and the early Christians. Prayer was particularly concerned with making requests to God (Phil. 4: 6, '...but in everything make your requests known to God in prayer and petition'). It is clearly one of the ways in which we co-operate with God. But such requests are not an attempt to make God do what *we* want him to do, nor are they an attempt to make God listen to us (Matt. 5: 7, 'In your prayers do not go babbling on like the heathen, who imagine that the more they say the more likely they are to be heard. Do not imitate them. Your Father knows what your needs are before you ask him'). Prayer of the right kind can never be selfish. Jesus himself taught that the fundamental request to God was that his will should be done (Matt. 6: 9, 'Thy name be hallowed, Thy Kingdom come, Thy will be done'). Similarly another early prayer is 'Marana tha', which means 'Come, O Lord!' (I. Cor. 16: 22)—a prayer for the coming of God's final kingdom and the fulfilment of his purposes. Paul asks too for the prayers of his hearers that he may play his part in the working out of these purposes (Eph. 6: 20). Prayer for others is one of the ways in which we can bring them God's power and help (2 Cor. 1: 11). Again, as in our present passage, another important kind of request was that God would give a deeper understanding of the Christian Gospel and its implications, so that one can move closer into line with God's mind and attitude (see also Col. 1: 9, 'We ask God that you may receive from him all wisdom and spiritual understanding...').

18–19*a*. There are three points where Christians are to have insight:

(i) Into the sureness of their hope. This is not a flimsy hoping for the best. It arises out of God's *call* into friendship with himself. It results from the conviction that God's cause will win the day, and that nothing in death or life can make a rift between us and his love, and that an even fuller and more satisfying life awaits us in the future.

(ii) Into the wonderful privileges they possess. *heritage* was used in the Old Testament to describe the blessings of the land of Canaan, and now describes the privilege of belonging among those who know the closeness of God's love in Jesus Christ.

(iii) Into the all-sufficiency of God's *power* to help and strengthen those who are committed to him. ✳

THE SOVEREIGNTY OF JESUS CHRIST

They are measured by his strength and the might which 19, 20 he exerted in Christ when he raised him from the dead, when he enthroned him at his right hand in the heavenly realms, far above all government and authority, all power 21 and dominion, and any title of sovereignty that can be named, not only in this age but in the age to come. He 22 put everything in subjection beneath his feet, and appointed him as supreme head to the church, which is 23 his body and as such holds within it the fullness of him who himself receives the entire fullness of God.

✳ The grounds for Christian confidence in God are now given.

19*b*–20. Christians' assurance about the future, about their status and God's 'resources' is not based on wishful thinking, but on human experience of how God *raised* Jesus *from the dead*. At the time of his crucifixion Jesus appeared to be crushed.

His earthly life was ended, and all that he claimed and stood for seemed to be finished. He also appeared to be a 'spent force', as the manner of his execution spelt in Jewish thought the curse of God (Deut. 21: 23, 'For he that is hanged is accursed of God'). But against the odds and probabilities, and almost against their own wills, the disciples had an experience of Jesus after his death that convinced them that his mission had not ended in failure. Unlike that of other people, his death had not ended his career. He was still a living force and power to be reckoned with, and had something to say to the world. In this 'come-back' of Jesus, God has set the seal of his approval on Jesus' work and life; he has given his demonstration that the forces which try to frustrate his purposes will not succeed. This 'break-through' means that Jesus is 'enthroned' as King. He is the point where God says to men: 'I am sovereign in my world, and loyalty to *me* is one that overrides all others.'

21. *government, authority, power* and *dominion* are ways of describing angelic powers or spirits, which were thought in Paul's day to have the world and the destiny of human beings in their grasp. Belief in these powers played upon people's superstitions and fears. Some were obsessed with the need to use magic and other devices to keep on the right side of them.

any title of sovereignty is in the Greek 'every name that is named'. In the world contemporary with Paul, a name was thought to carry power with it, and reverence was paid to the names of gods, demons and heroes. In Jesus Christ God has said No! to all these claimants for the control of human life.

this age was the Jewish way of describing the present state of the world and society which was in the grip of forces opposed to God. But the Jews looked forward to the world as it one day would be, with God given his proper place; and they called this *the age to come*. Paul is therefore saying that the only loyalty that matters now or at any time is loyalty to Jesus. See also Rom. 8: 31–39.

22–23. The opening words are based on Psalm 8: 6 ('Thou hast put all things under his feet'). This originally described

God's placing of the creation in the hands of man. It was then seen to be a suitable way of describing the work of Jesus. In him God has demonstrated that he will reign and be 'all in all'. At the moment, God's sovereignty is not accepted everywhere; it is however to be observed in *the church*.

In the Old Testament, *church* or 'congregation' describes the Jews, as God's people, who are in a special relationship with himself (e.g. 1 Chron. 29: 20, 'And all the congregation blessed the Lord'). The same word is now applied to Christians, who are God's people, i.e. those who have been brought into closer fellowship with God through the work of Jesus Christ.

head and *body* describe the 'one who controls' and the 'sphere controlled' (see below, p. 111). The rest of the passage is difficult, but the translation in the text gives the most probable sense. Jesus as God's Word or Wisdom *receives the entire fullness of God*, i.e. he is part of God's being and therefore in him human beings are confronted with God's being and life. In turn the church *holds the fullness* of Jesus in the sense of being his sphere of influence and his 'operations centre'. ✻

THE LIFE OUT OF TUNE WITH GOD

Time was when you were dead in your sins and wicked- **2** ness, when you followed the evil ways of this present age, ₂ when you obeyed the commander of the spiritual powers of the air, the spirit now at work among God's rebel subjects. We too were of their number: we all lived ₃ our lives in sensuality, and obeyed the promptings of our own instincts and notions. In our natural condition we, like the rest, lay under the dreadful judgement of God.

✻ There are different levels at which people can live. There is the higher level of trying to keep in step with God and his purposes, and there is the lower level where God is ignored and 'self' looms large. Paul now describes the second level, at which those addressed had once lived.

1. *sins and wickedness* is a way of describing rebellion against God and rejection of his purposes and will. Human beings are created to serve God, and in obeying him the full purpose of life is found. To be out of tune or out of step with this purpose can therefore be described as death. Paul had similarly described himself as *dead* when he was unable to live up to God's commandments (e.g. Rom. 7: 9, 'but when the commandment came, sin sprang to life and I died').

2. The Jews believed that the *present* state of the world and human behaviour left a lot to be desired. They faced their situation not with cynicism but with the hope that God would end the present bad state of things and set up a new order in which he would reign and his will would be done. Some of the present troubles were also traced to the influence of certain superhuman forces of evil (here called *the commander of the spiritual powers of the air*). The existence of such powers should not necessarily be ruled out; but the important idea behind such belief is that men have deadly enemies to overcome, sometimes of their own creating: such as selfishness, envy, hatred and various kinds of prejudice.

3. *We* means that Paul and those addressed had all once been in this same position. This 'lower level' of existence is now further seen as a 'do as you please' kind of attitude. *sensuality* describes the pull in human beings that draws them away from God to thoughts of self. *in our natural condition* means without the help and intervention of God.

we lay under the dreadful judgement of God is in the Greek: 'we were children of wrath'. God is righteous and demands righteousness, and so human sin and all that is evil must meet with his opposition and condemnation. This reaction of God is described in the Old Testament as his 'wrath' or 'anger' (e.g. Ps. 106: 29, 'Thus they provoked him to anger with their doings'). Therefore, to be 'children of wrath' means to be living at loggerheads with God.   ✳

GOD PUTS MATTERS RIGHT

But God, rich in mercy, for the great love he bore us, 4
brought us to life with Christ even when we were dead 5
in our sins; it is by his grace you are saved. And in union 6
with Christ Jesus he raised us up and enthroned us with
him in the heavenly realms, so that he might display in 7
the ages to come how immense are the resources of his
grace, and how great his kindness to us in Christ Jesus.
For it is by his grace you are saved, through trusting 8
him; it is not your own doing. It is God's gift, not a 9
reward for work done. There is nothing for anyone to
boast of. For we are God's handiwork, created in Christ 10
Jesus to devote ourselves to the good deeds for which
God has designed us.

* Paul now tells us how God makes a higher level of life
possible.

4. God's *mercy* or *love* both describe his sense of responsibility
for the human race. These qualities of God were known
already to the Old Testament writers (e.g. Ps. 145: 8, 'The
Lord is gracious, and full of compassion; Slow to anger, and
of great mercy. The Lord is good to all; And his tender mercies are over all his works'). God's love has, however, been
experienced at its closest in the mission of Jesus Christ. We
notice that it is a love resulting in practical action.

5. Central features of Jesus' life were his obedience to the
will of God, his selflessness and his love for his fellow human
beings. This is the higher level of life, and the claims made for
it are shown to be justified by the resurrection of Jesus. We are
therefore *brought to life* in the sense that the possibility of our
rising to this new level is held out through our relationship
with the risen and triumphant Jesus. This rescue operation can
be traced to God's *grace* or favour.

6. Jesus' earthly life and his acceptance of death were a triumph of absolute confidence in God. The 'come-back' of Jesus at his resurrection and his enthronement as King showed that such a God-centred way of living was not misplaced. Therefore, to be *in union with Christ Jesus* means to be *raised up* and *enthroned* with Jesus in the sense of being committed to the God-centred way of life.

in the heavenly realms: the higher level of life has God as its focal point.

7. *in the ages to come* might mean the future or future generations, but more probably refers to 'the age to come', the era when God reigns and calls his world to a final reckoning. Then Christians (*a*) will be important witnesses to what the love (*grace*) of God has achieved in men's lives, and (*b*) will have an even greater vision of what they owe to God.

8. Again God's loving initiative is stressed. *trusting him* means grasping the lifeline that God holds out to us in Jesus Christ.

9. The Christian's reconciliation with God is not something earned by merit, and the result of bargaining. It is a *gift*, because God offers his love and friendship, and asks us to accept it. Paul is here dampening any tendency to pride in those addressed, and also has in mind the Jewish idea that friendship with God was something that was *a reward for work done*.

In the Letters to the Galatians and to the Romans, Paul argues strongly that it is impossible to gain a right relationship with God by means of one's own good deeds, because we fall short of what he requires of us (e.g. Rom. 3: 23, 'For all alike have sinned, and are deprived of the divine splendour, and all are justified by God's free grace alone...').

10. God is here seen as the artist or craftsman who has *created* our present status with himself. It is made possible *in Christ Jesus* through being linked to him and what he has achieved. But out of this new relationship of love must spring the responsibility for *good deeds*, i.e. action and conduct worthy of God. ✻

A REMINDER ABOUT THE PAST

Remember then your former condition: you, Gentiles as 11
you are outwardly, you, 'the uncircumcised' so called
by those who are called 'the circumcised' (but only with
reference to an outward rite)—you were at that time 12
separate from Christ, strangers to the community of
Israel, outside God's covenants and the promise that goes
with them. Your world was a world without hope and
without God. But now in union with Christ Jesus you 13
who once were far off have been brought near through
the shedding of Christ's blood. For he is himself our 14
peace. Gentiles and Jews, he has made the two one, and
in his own body of flesh and blood has broken down
the enmity which stood like a dividing wall between
them; for he annulled the law with its rules and regula- 15
tions, so as to create out of the two a single new humanity
in himself, thereby making peace. This was his purpose, 16
to reconcile the two in a single body to God through
the cross, on which he killed the enmity.

✫ Paul's hearers had belonged to the non-Jewish world. He sees the human race before the coming of Jesus Christ divided into two main groups: the Jewish nation and the rest of mankind. The Jews were 'different' not because of any racial superiority but because God had made himself more intimately known to this nation in readiness for revealing himself to the whole world. The Jewish religion had a refinement about it, compared with other religions. When a small nation has 'something special' about it in this way, it points to the conclusion that this is not the result of chance but is part of a plan by which God is educating his world.

11. The *Gentiles* or 'the nations' was the way in which the

Jews referred to non-Jews. Physical circumcision was demanded of all male Jewish children and was considered to be the special sign that God had chosen the Jews to be his people. (Gen. 17: 10, 'This is my covenant, which ye shall keep between me and you and thy seed after thee; every male among you shall be circumcised'). Therefore *the uncircumcised* became a term used to describe those who did not belong to the Jewish nation. It could become an expression of abuse, when the Jews became obsessed with their own privileges, and when they were persecuted by other nations.

12. *separate from Christ*, i.e. not yet reconciled to God through the work of Jesus. *Israel* here means God's specially chosen people, the Jews. God's dealings with the Jews were based on special *covenants* or agreements, especially the one made at the time of the deliverance from Egypt (Exod. 24). This covenant created a deep impression on the Jews, and appeal was made to it by Old Testament writers (e.g. Jer. 34: 13, 'Thus saith the Lord, the God of Israel: I made a covenant with your fathers in the day that I brought them forth out of the land of Egypt...'). This special arrangement between God and the Jews brought with it the *promise* that Israel would play an important part in God's plans (e.g. Gen. 18: 18, 'seeing that Abraham shall surely become a great and mighty nation, and all the nations of the earth shall be blessed in him'). The people addressed here were out of touch with the true God and so were *without hope*.

13. Jesus is the 'meeting-point' with God for all mankind. To bring people together can be a costly business. To give human beings the chance of coming closer to God involved *the shedding of Christ's blood*. Jesus continued to love people even when it resulted in his execution by crucifixion; he showed how much God was in real earnest. At the 'last supper' Jesus saw his coming death as a way of bringing all into fellowship with God (Mk. 14: 24, 'This is my blood of the covenant, shed for many', i.e. 'for all'). The Gentiles had been *far off* in the sense of being out of touch with God and his purposes,

just as the Jews were sometimes described as being 'near' to
God (e.g. Ps. 148: 14, 'Even of the children of Israel, a people
near to him').

14. *peace* in the New Testament usually means the harmony
that Jesus has brought between God and man. As a result he
is the common meeting-ground where human divisions are
broken down, and so is *our peace*. This is seen in miniature in
Jesus' *own body of flesh and blood*, i.e. in his earthly life. In his
earthly ministry he made no distinctions between the people
that he loved and helped; they included the scum of Jewish
society (e.g. Luke 7: 36–50), and non-Jews, such as the Roman
centurion (Matt. 8: 5) and the Samaritan woman (John 4: 8).

The picture of *the dividing wall* may have been suggested
by the balustrade or barrier which marked that point in the
Jewish Temple at Jerusalem beyond which non-Jews were
not supposed to go. Notices were put up to give warning to
this effect. One of these has been discovered and reads: 'No
alien to pass within the fence and enclosure round the temple.
Whoever shall be taken shall be responsible to himself alone
for the death which will ensue.'

15. *the law* is the so-called Law of Moses contained in the
first five books of the Old Testament, i.e. Genesis, Exodus,
Leviticus, Numbers and Deuteronomy. It consists of Jewish
traditions about their early history, and of religious regulations, some of which may go back to the lawgiver Moses. A
lot of this material had been passed on orally and had been
written down at various periods. The books came into their
present form between 500 and 400 B.C., and were meant to be
the basis of the life of the Jewish community in Palestine as
reformed by Nehemiah and Ezra in the period 460–397 B.C.
The main theme of this law is that God created the world, that
human beings rebelled against him, and that the Jews were
given a special part to play in God's plan for winning the
world back to himself. This was particularly shown in the
miraculous deliverance of the Jews from slavery in Egypt and
the covenant made with them through Moses on Mount Sinai.

The law's many *rules and regulations* were intended to keep the Jewish nation separate and its belief in the one God safe, until God could make himself more widely known. Jesus Christ is the point of union where human beings can become a *single new humanity*.

16. The *single body* is, first of all, Jesus himself, the common point of meeting, and then the Church, which rises above divisions of nationality, colour, class or birth and is all-inclusive. *The cross* has become by this time a phrase which in itself suggests the love of God to all mankind. *enmity* is the barrier between Jew and non-Jew. ✶

THE CHANGED POSITION OF THE GENTILES

17 So he came and proclaimed the good news: peace to you who were far off, and peace to those who were near
18 by; for through him we both alike have access to the
19 Father in the one Spirit. Thus you are no longer aliens in a foreign land, but fellow-citizens with God's people,
20 members of God's household. You are built upon the foundation laid by the apostles and prophets, and Christ
21 Jesus himself is the foundation-stone. In him the whole building is bonded together and grows into a holy
22 temple in the Lord. In him you too are being built with all the rest into a spiritual dwelling for God.

✶ Through the new order brought by Jesus Christ, Jew and Gentile have equal place and privilege in God's people. Paul likens the Church to a building and describes the kind of building it is to be.

17. *came* probably refers both to the earthly mission of Jesus and to the work of the early Church. *the good news* is a special way of describing God's rescue operation (see above on 1: 13). In his use of *far off* and *near* Paul probably has Isaiah

57: 19 in mind ('Peace, peace, to him that is far off and to him that is near, saith the Lord'). By this time *the good news* had been preached to the Gentiles (the *far off*), and the Jews (the *near by*) over a wide area in the East and in Europe.

18. *peace* also brings with it *access* to God, a word that could describe one's introduction into the presence of a king. Jesus is perhaps thought of here as the officer in the king's court who makes the presentation. To be with a person can mean that this person has an influence upon us; so to be introduced into the presence of God means to receive his *Spirit* or influence into our life. This is the common experience of Jew and Gentile within the Christian Church.

19. In the Greek city-state there was a distinction between the body of *citizens*, who formed the Assembly and had a vote on policy, and the resident *aliens*, the people from abroad, who had no such rights. The Gentiles are now full citizens of God's city-state. In the Old Testament God's house, in the sense of *household*, is used in the phrase 'house of Israel' to describe God's people (e.g. Psalm 135: 18, 'O house of Israel, bless ye the Lord').

20. *household* leads to the picture of the Church as a building. The *apostles* (see above on 1: 1) and *prophets* rank first among the leaders of the early Church (see 1 Cor. 12: 28). The prophets had a special gift from God to give guidance to the Christian communities, and to declare God's will. For example, in Acts 13: 1-4, it is the prophets who declare God's will about the first big missionary journey, and down the ages the Church has produced her prophets. In the translation as we have it in the text, the *foundation laid* is the preaching of the Gospel together with the founding and guiding of the Christian communities. Another way of taking the passage is to see the apostles and prophets as the *foundation*, i.e. as leaders of the Church. the *foundation-stone* or (as sometimes translated) 'keystone' has been explained as the stone which was in the centre of the archway and locked some ancient buildings together; it is more likely to have been an important stone in the

foundation. In either case the point being made is that the Church owes everything to Jesus and is entirely dependent on him.

21. *the whole building* means the Church throughout the world. An ancient building would be held or *bonded together* by the skill of the builder in fitting the different stones together, and especially in obtaining the correct balance in the arches. The church is composed of different communities and people of different kinds, and can only be *bonded together* by a common allegiance to Jesus Christ and by recognition that he alone is the source of the Church's power. But it is a building that cannot be static; it must be growing more and more fit to carry out the task for which it exists. Paul therefore goes on to show us what kind of building is in process of construction. The Church is to become *a holy temple.* A temple had important associations for people at this time. For example, the Jewish temple at Jerusalem was thought of as the place where God met his people and was worshipped by them; here too the worshipper was faced with God's claim upon his allegiance. So the Christian Church is to grow into a *temple* or centre of worship, i.e. is to become a community in whose life and behaviour the power and presence of God are to be seen and his will acknowledged. In this way the Church will be a 'display centre' challenging the world with God's claim on human allegiance. Such a temple is *holy* as set apart and given over to the service of God.

If instead of *the whole building* we read 'every structure' (as in the footnote to the N.E.B.) it will refer to each community of Christians.

22. Those addressed form a section of this building, and so have their part to play in making the Church a *dwelling for God*, i.e. the sphere where his will is acknowledged and carried out. *spiritual* means that it is only 'in the Spirit', i.e. with God's power, that such an end is achieved. ✳

THE SPECIAL INSIGHT OF THE APOSTLES
AND PROPHETS

With this in mind I make my prayer, I, Paul, who in the **3**
cause of you Gentiles am now the prisoner of Christ
Jesus—for surely you have heard how God has assigned 2
the gift of his grace to me for your benefit. It was by a 3
revelation that his secret was made known to me. I have
already written a brief account of this, and by reading it 4
you may perceive that I understand the secret of Christ.
In former generations this was not disclosed to the human 5
race; but now it has been revealed by inspiration to his
dedicated apostles and prophets, that through the 6
Gospel the Gentiles are joint heirs with the Jews, part of
the same body, sharers together in the promise made in
Christ Jesus.

✴ Like the Mystery religions, the Church has her leaders,
who can explain divine secrets.

1. Paul begins a prayer which breaks off and is only completed at 3: 14. He will not admit that he is the *prisoner* of the
Roman Emperor, Nero; he is the captive of only one person,
Jesus. His life was under the latter's direction, and it was the
preaching of the Gospel that had eventually led to his being
taken into protective custody by the Romans (Acts 21); to
his appeal to the Emperor's court (Acts 25: 11–12); and to his
journey to Rome (Acts 27–28).

2. Even if many of those addressed had not seen Paul, yet it
was due to his efforts that they had heard the Gospel. *how God
has assigned the gift of his grace* means literally 'the stewardship
of God's grace', which can mean (*a*) 'the office of apostle
that is mine as the result of God's favour' or (*b*) 'the showing of
God's favour'. In either case Paul underlines that his privileges
are not due to any merit in himself.

3. *By revelation* refers to the special experience that Paul had of the risen Jesus (see Acts 9: 1–19; Gal. 1: 15–16). God's *secret* into which Paul was let was (*a*) that Jesus was no impostor but the true agent of God and (*b*) that in Jesus God had given the assurance of his love, which was to be conveyed to all men.

4. By *this* is most naturally meant the *revelation*, and the *account mentioned* may have been one specially written by Paul to show how the big change in his attitude to Jesus Christ took place. We know that Paul, though convinced of his commission as an apostle, was sensitive about his earlier persecution of the church (e.g. 1 Cor. 15: 9, 'for I had persecuted the church of God and am therefore inferior to all other apostles—indeed not fit to be called an apostle'). Paul's previous hostility aroused doubts and suspicions in some Christians' minds about the genuineness of his call to be an apostle. It has indeed been conjectured that this suspicion and distrust form the 'sharp pain in my body' to which Paul refers in 2 Cor. 12: 7. It is highly likely that Paul had issued a manifesto of some kind to explain his position. In it Paul had, it seems, also given an explanation of the Gospel.

5–6. An important part of God's plan is that in Jesus Christ the barrier between Jew and Gentile is removed. Previously it had not been *disclosed* to the human race how God would provide a meeting-point for Jews and Gentiles, though in some Jewish writings the Gentiles are seen as having a definite place in God's purposes (e.g. Isa. 2: 2, 'And it shall come to pass in the latter days, that the mountain of the Lord's house shall be established in the top of the mountains, and shall be exalted above the hills; and all nations shall flow into it'). Similarly the Jews, especially those in the Jewish colonies scattered over the Roman world, tried to commend their faith to the Gentiles and bring them to believe in the one God.

That Jesus and his gospel had relevance to the Gentiles was *revealed by inspiration to his dedicated apostles and prophets* in various ways. The Risen Jesus had spoken of this to his disciples (Acts 1: 8, 'And you will bear witness for me in Jerusalem, and all over Judaea and Samaria, and away to the ends of the earth'). The vision that the Apostle Peter saw while at Joppa also convinced him that in God's sight the Gentiles were as valuable as the Jews (Acts 10: 1-16, and we may note especially 10: 28, 'He [Peter] said to them, "I need not tell you that a Jew is forbidden by his religion to visit or associate with a man of another race; yet God has shown me clearly that I must not call any man profane or unclean"'). Similarly, under the guidance of the prophets (see above on 2: 20), the Church at Antioch took the big step of commissioning the apostles Barnabas and Paul to undertake missionary work farther afield, which would include preaching the gospel to Gentiles as well as Jews (Acts 13: 1-3). It was the persecution which followed the death of the first Christian martyr, Stephen, that supplied the impetus to the first preaching of the gospel to non-Jews (Acts 11: 19-21, where we are told that this great step forward took place at Antioch). After this start and the clear evidence given to Peter that he was to preach the gospel to non-Jews, the big point at issue was not whether Gentiles should be admitted to the Church's membership, but the terms on which this should take place.

The N.E.B. translation *the promise made in Christ Jesus* is a reference to the offer of a right relationship with God brought by Jesus. But another, and preferable, translation would be: 'the Gentiles are in Christ Jesus joint heirs with the Jews, part of the same body, sharers together in the promise.' The *promise* is then that made to the Jews of a better order of things in which God was better known. *in Christ Jesus* stresses that he is the point of union of humanity. ✳

PAUL'S SERVICE FOR THE GOSPEL

Such is the gospel of which I was made a minister, by 7 God's gift, bestowed unmerited on me in the working of his power. To me, who am less than the least of all 8

God's people, he has granted of his grace the privilege of proclaiming to the Gentiles the good news of the un-
9 fathomable riches of Christ, and of bringing to light how
10 this hidden purpose was to be put into effect. It was hidden for long ages in God the creator of the universe, in order that now, through the church, the wisdom of God in all its varied forms might be made known to the
11 rulers and authorities in the realms of heaven. This is in accord with his age-long purpose, which he achieved in
12 Christ Jesus our Lord. In him we have access to God
13 with freedom, in the confidence born of trust in him. I beg you, then, not to lose heart over my sufferings for you: indeed, they are your glory.

✴ Paul, unworthy as he is, is privileged to proclaim the good news brought to the world in Jesus Christ. The church is a witness to the prior claims of God over all other claims on human allegiance. In Jesus, God has come very close to us, and so calls forth our confidence. Paul's present sufferings are no cause for despair. Compare this section with Col. 1: 23–27.

7. *minister*: a word also used of the office of deacon (e.g. Phil. 1: 1, '. . . to all those of God's people. . . including their bishops and deacons'). Here it describes one who gives himself to the service of Jesus. Paul's high status (as he always stresses) is due to no merit on his own part, and his office can only be carried out by God's *power* (see also 1 Cor. 15: 10, 'However, by God's grace I am what I am'). *less than the least* is Paul's way of expressing his utter unworthiness for his position as apostle (see 1 Cor. 15: 9, '. . . for I had persecuted the church of God and am therefore inferior to all other apostles'). It is sometimes thought that Paul would not have used such an exaggerated term of himself. But here it offsets the claims that Paul has been making for himself, and makes it clear that his understanding of the gospel is something owed to God.

8–9. Paul's work did not exclude Jews from its scope (1 Cor. 9: 20, 'To the Jews I became like a Jew, to win Jews'). But he saw himself as having a special commission to non-Jews (Acts 9: 15; Gal. 1: 16). *unfathomable*, because God's approach to us in Jesus Christ never ceases to cause wonder, and has a depth of meaning that can never be exhausted. The *hidden purpose* was *put into effect* through the totally unexpected —the cross and resurrection of Jesus Christ.

10. God as *creator* is responsible for the life-giving forces that have brought the universe and human beings into existence; he also, at the right moment, gives redirection to that which is not going according to plan. The *rulers and authorities* may have been for Paul real superhuman forces of evil, claiming to dominate human life and keep God out. They stand for all the forces that try to wreck and undermine human existence, i.e. the sense of insecurity and fear, the absorption in material things, rivalry, race-hatred, selfishness. The *church* stands witness to God's *wisdom*, his scheme for human living, and so gives the counterblast to these destructive forces.

11. God's *age-long purpose* was to restore human beings to himself.

12. One of the worst enemies of man is a feeling of insecurity and that the world is against him. The Gospel brings the *freedom* or sense of security that comes from knowing that this is a friendly world with a God at the heart of it whom it is possible to approach as a trustworthy friend.

13. Paul's *suffering*, i.e. his imprisonment, might suggest that God is not to be trusted. Paul is confident that somehow even these sufferings are helping those addressed (*for you*), and bringing nearer the time when they would share in the *glory* of God's Kingdom (see also Col. 1: 24, 'It is now my happiness to suffer for you. This is my way of helping to complete, in my poor human flesh, the full tale of Christ's afflictions still be endured...'). ✻

PAUL'S PRAYER

14 With this in mind, then, I kneel in prayer to the Father,
15 from whom every family in heaven and on earth takes
16 its name, that out of the treasures of his glory he may
grant you strength and power through his Spirit in your
17 inner being, that through faith Christ may dwell in your
hearts in love. With deep roots and firm foundations,
18 may you be strong to grasp, with all God's people, what
is the breadth and length and height and depth of the
19 love of Christ, and to know it, though it is beyond
knowledge. So may you attain to fullness of being, the
fullness of God himself.

20   Now to him who is able to do immeasurably more than
21 all we can ask or conceive, by the power which is at work
among us, to him be glory in the church and in Christ
Jesus from generation to generation evermore! Amen.

* Paul now continues with the prayer that he began at 3: 1.
We saw earlier, at 1: 17, that the purpose of prayer is to draw
closer to God and his will, and here Paul's prayer is that his
hearers may more and more appreciate the love of Jesus and
respond to it.

14–15. *the Father*: Jesus had taught his disciples to begin their
prayer with 'Our Father' (Matt. 6: 9), which describes God
as one who is accessible and has a loving responsibility for the
human race. In the Greek there is a play on words between
Father (*pater*) and *family* (*patria*).

every family in heaven is best taken as describing God's
angels, who were thought of by the Jews as forming God's
heavenly court, and as being intermediaries between God and
his world; they are sometimes described as arranged in
families. The families *on earth* are the Christian congregations.

Angels and Christians here form the body of God's loyal servants. The linking of the heavenly and earthly families in this way receives some light from the Dead Sea Scrolls. These documents tell of the life and beliefs of a Jewish community or sect which had its headquarters at Qumran near the Dead Sea and belongs to the period of the first century B.C. and the first century A.D. Part of one of its hymns stresses the community's sense of union with the angels: 'Thou hast cleansed a perverse spirit of great sin that it may stand with the host of the Holy Ones, and that it may enter into community with the congregation of the Sons of Heaven' (Hymn 5, *The Dead Sea Scrolls in English*, G. Vermes, Penguin Books, p. 148). *takes its name* means that all these families receive their status and strength from God.

16–17a. God's *glory* is in the Bible often connected with God's making himself known and coming to the help of man (e.g. Ps. 90: 16, 'Let thy work appear unto thy servants, And thy glory upon their children'). God's *Spirit* is his activity in giving people 'extra thrust' to carry out his will. When people are fully behind their leader and ready to follow him to the end, they embody the spirit of the leader and in a way he dwells in them. So Paul prays that *Christ may dwell in your hearts*. Such a union will be seen in the *love* that Christians have for Jesus Christ, and for their fellow human beings.

17b–19. Paul's prayer is that Christians may be like a mature tree that has thrust down *deep roots*, or like a building that has a solid deep-dug *foundation*. We may compare the words of Jesus in Matthew 7: 24–25 ('What then of the man who hears these words of mine and acts upon them? He is like a man who had the sense to build his house on rock'). To achieve this, they have to take into their very bones *the love of Christ* in all its dimensions. That self-giving love of the Son of God in dying for human beings is *beyond knowledge*, i.e. the wonder of it can never really be appreciated.

Response to someone's love can bring out the best in people; so the Christian's response to the love of Jesus Christ will bring out the character in which love is the central feature. In this way Jesus' disciples will be 'sons of the Most High' (Luke 6: 35) because such love is part of the *fullness* or perfection of God himself. It is also possible to translate as in the N.E.B. footnote: 'the fullness that God requires', i.e. the perfection demanded by God.

20–21. Paul ends his prayer and this part of the letter with an act of praise to God who is able to achieve his ends. What Paul has prayed for can only be achieved by the *power* of God. Men's vision of God's power to effect his purposes is far too small, but something of it can be seen in what God has done in the Church and in the lives of Christians (*the power at work among us*).

in the church. Paul begins with *the church* because it is here that God's kingship and majesty are acknowledged in the present, and confront the world. But the Church's witness is dependent on *Christ Jesus*, in whom God's nature and being are revealed. The order *church/Christ Jesus* stresses that the honour of Jesus is in the hands of the Church; for the impression of him that people receive is that given by the Church and individual Christians.

from generation to generation evermore! Amen. The usual way of ending an act of praise. The only sure and lasting factor in life is God himself. ✳

THE TRUE UNITY

4 I entreat you, then—I, a prisoner for the Lord's sake: as
2 God has called you, live up to your calling. Be humble always and gentle, and patient too. Be forbearing with
3 one another and charitable. Spare no effort to make fast with bonds of peace the unity which the Spirit gives.
4 There is one body and one Spirit, as there is also one
5 hope held out in God's call to you; one Lord, one faith,
6 one baptism; one God and Father of all, who is over all and through all and in all.

✲ The central point for understanding human life is the love of God revealed in Jesus Christ. The practical implications of this belief have now to be faced. As often, the second part of the letter is devoted to this theme. We may compare Rom. 12: 1, 'Therefore, my brothers, I implore you by God's mercy to offer your very selves to him.'

1. *then*, i.e. because of God's 'outreach' to us in Jesus. Paul's advice is not based on pure theory; his loyalty to Jesus Christ has been at the cost of imprisonment and peril. God's call to be in fellowship with him is an honour, but when accepted makes demands.

2. *humble* does not mean a cringing attitude and a false belittlement of oneself. It is rather setting a correct value on oneself, as one intended to be dependent on God and to do his will.

gentle may misleadingly suggest timidity and lack of the courage to hold to one's convictions; it should either be taken as another word for *humble*, or it may mean 'courteous, considerate towards others'.

patient (sometimes also translated 'slow to anger') is a quality of God stressed in the Old Testament (e.g. Num. 14: 18, 'The Lord is slow to anger, and plenteous in mercy'). Here it means a refusal to be hasty with our fellow human beings, and an attempt to understand them and sympathize with them. The same applies to *forbearing*, which is not just putting up with someone in an intolerant way, but involves being *charitable*, i.e. showing a love that puts itself out for other people.

3. This verse and what follows are often thought to stress the need for unity among the different Christian communities, which were perhaps drifting away from each other. But *unity* in the rest of Ephesians is very much concerned with Jesus Christ as the point of unity, where the solution to human life can be found (in contrast with the false 'philosophies of life' mentioned below in 4: 14). So here the meaning may be that Christians are to hold *fast* to this *unity* and work out the

implications of it in their lives. It is a unity made clear to men by God's *Spirit* (see above on 3: 4–6).

peace here means the reconciliation between God and man, effected in Jesus.

4. In the first century, as today, there were many recipes and solutions for coming to terms with life. There were a large number of gods or divine powers, and many religious sects or societies (e.g. the Mystery religions) through membership of which one's future could be secured. But for Paul there is the *one* solution, and *one* society or *body*, the Church, where the true answer to life is found. In the same way there is only one divine power at work in the world, the *Spirit* of God. The Christian also has a future—the *one hope*, the only hope that is valid—certified by the life, death and resurrection of Jesus Christ. This *hope* is that God will work his purposes for the world; that nothing at all, including physical death, can separate us from the love of God; and that God has in store for us a full life of fellowship with him. Such *hope* is purely the result of God's goodness seen in his *call*, i.e. into friendship with himself.

5. In the first century A.D. the many cults and Mystery religions each had its own head or lord. But for Paul there is only *one Lord*, Jesus, through whom we are put right with the God of the whole world and gain the security that matters. This is attained through the *one faith*, i.e. personal allegiance to Jesus, the loyalty that matters. Such *faith* receives its outward expression in the rite of *baptism* (see below, p. 73), by which admittance to Christ's family is achieved. It is the *one* rite that matters, as opposed to the rites of admittance to other religions.

6. Finally the unity of the universe is stressed by mention of the *one God* (in contrast to the belief in many gods, a feature of the contemporary world).

But *Father* describes this God as one who is not an abstract principle, but as one who has a personal love and care for his world. He is *over all* as the source of creation, but is *through all* and *in all*, as being deeply involved and interested in it.

With the emphasis on the *one God* and the *one Lord* we may compare 1 Cor. 8: 6 ('...yet for us there is one God, the Father, from whom all being comes, towards whom we move; and there is one Lord, Jesus Christ, through whom all things came to be, and we through him').

This section calls for two further comments:

(1) In verses 4–6 Paul may be quoting from a kind of creed or statement of belief with which his hearers were familiar. The New Testament contains a number of what seem to be short summaries or statements of Christian belief which were already in use by the early Church and which are quoted by Paul and other writers. Among these is the short statement 'Jesus is Lord' or 'Jesus is the Son of God' (Rom. 10: 9; 1 John 2: 22), words in which a candidate at baptism probably expressed his allegiance to Jesus. Another example of part of an early Christian creed is that quoted by Paul in 1 Cor. 15: 3 ff. ('that Christ died for our sins, in accordance with the scriptures; that he was buried; that he was raised to life on the third day, according to the scriptures'). A convenient summary like this might well have been used in the training of candidates for baptism. Other statements of belief sound more like hymns, such as that in Philippians 2: 6–11 ('For the divine nature was his from the first; yet he did not think to snatch at equality with God, but made himself nothing, assuming the nature of a slave. Bearing the human likeness, revealed in human shape, he humbled himself, and in obedience accepted even death—death on a cross. Therefore God raised him to the heights and bestowed on him the name above all names, that at the name of Jesus every knee should bow—in heaven, on earth, and in the depths—and every tongue confess, "Jesus Christ is Lord", to the glory of God the Father'). This is almost certainly an early Christian hymn in honour of Jesus, and the same applies to 1 Timothy 3: 16, where we have a hymn-like creed:

> 'He who was manifested in the body,
> vindicated in the spirit,
> seen by angels;
> who was proclaimed among the nations,
> believed in throughout the world,
> glorified in high heaven.'

We can imagine such hymns as these being used in the worship of the Christian congregations, and they may be included among the 'hymns' mentioned in Eph. 5: 18. We may here compare the use in Jewish worship of the Old Testament Psalms, some of which are recitals of the mighty things that God has done for the Jewish nation (e.g. Psalm 106: 9–10, 'He rebuked the Red Sea also, and it was dried up: So he led them through the depths, as through a wilderness').

(2) In this short creed the thought begins with the observable Church where God's *Spirit* is at work, and passes to the *one Lord*, the Risen Jesus, who founded the Church, and through whom the *one God and Father of all* has been made known. We notice that the Spirit, the Lord Jesus, and God the Father are placed here in close proximity to each other. This is common in the New Testament (e.g. 1 Cor. 12: 4–6, 'There are varieties of gifts, but the same Spirit. There are varieties of service, but the same Lord. There are many forms of work, but all of them, in all men, are the work of the same God'). Sometimes the same happens in passages where God's part in the rite of baptism is referred to (e.g. 2 Cor. 1: 21–22, 'And if you and we belong to Christ, guaranteed as his and anointed, it is all God's doing; it is God also who has set his seal upon us, and as a pledge of what is to come has given the Spirit to dwell in our hearts'; and Matthew 28: 19, 'baptize men everywhere in the name of the Father and the Son and the Holy Spirit'). Statements such as these are evidence of the new experience of God that had come to the early followers of Jesus. As Jews they

believed in the one God, the Father. But another important factor—Jesus—had come into their lives. After his resurrection they felt impelled to give him an allegiance that was normally reserved for God alone. There was also another experience to be taken into account. The early Christians had received a new power in their lives, which they traced to the Holy Spirit of God. The nature of the Spirit's activity was not at first too closely defined, but there was a tendency to see it as a personal activity (e.g. Rom. 8: 26, 'In the same way the Spirit comes to the aid of our weakness'). This belief in God the Father, the Lord Jesus, and the Holy Spirit had somehow to be fitted into their other belief that God was one. The attempt to do justice to this new experience of God, and to achieve a satisfactory definition of it, occupied the attention of the church during the first centuries of its existence. It led to the formulation of the doctrine of the Trinity, as given for instance in the statement of belief known as the *Quicunque Vult*, which probably dates to the fifth century A.D. ('...we worship one God in Trinity, and the Trinity in Unity; Neither confusing the Persons: nor dividing the substance. For there is one Person of the Father, another of the Son: another of the Holy Spirit; But the Godhead of the Father, and of the Son, and of the Holy Spirit is all one: the glory equal, the majesty coeternal'). ✻

HOW THE CHURCH CAN DEVELOP

But each of us has been given his gift, his due portion 7 of Christ's bounty. Therefore Scripture says: 8

> 'He ascended into the heights
> With captives in his train;
> He gave gifts to men.'

Now, the word 'ascended' implies that he also de- 9 scended to the lowest level, down to the very earth. He 10

who descended is no other than he who ascended far
above all heavens, so that he might fill the universe.
11 And these were his gifts: some to be apostles, some
12 prophets, some evangelists, some pastors and teachers, to
equip God's people for work in his service, to the building
13 up of the body of Christ. So shall we all at last attain to
the unity inherent in our faith and our knowledge of the
14 Son of God—to mature manhood, measured by nothing
less than the full stature of Christ. We are no longer to
be children, tossed by the waves and whirled about by
every fresh gust of teaching, dupes of crafty rogues and
15 their deceitful schemes. No, let us speak the truth in
16 love; so shall we fully grow up into Christ. He is the
head, and on him the whole body depends. Bonded and
knit together by every constituent joint, the whole frame
grows through the due activity of each part, and builds
itself up in love.

* To help the Church to be a fit instrument for God's
purposes, and to help all Christians to play their proper part
in the service of God, certain Christians are equipped by
God with special gifts or powers that qualify them as leaders.

7. The Church has to work out the implications of believing that Jesus is the 'central point' of human life, and to
witness to this belief. For this purpose everyone has been
given special gifts. These are seen as *the due portion of Christ's
bounty*, i.e. the Risen Jesus gives to each member of his
Church a gift suitable for making a contribution to God's
service. An instructive commentary on this verse is the whole
of 1 Cor. 12, where Jesus is likened to an organism with his
followers as its parts, each having a function to perform
(e.g. verse 12, 'For Christ is like a single body with its many
limbs and organs, which, many as they are, together make up
one body').

8. The *Scripture* quoted is Psalm 68, 18:

> 'Thou didst ascend the high mount,
> Leading captives in thy train
> And receiving gifts among men.'   (R.S.V.)

Paul quotes the passage with slight alterations, which may mean that he is following a Jewish paraphrase. The early Christians thought the Old Testament important because it told how God had prepared for the coming of Jesus Christ. It was therefore natural, as here, to see passages of the Old Testament foreshadowing him. Originally the Psalm described the Jewish king's triumphal procession to the newly conquered hill of Jerusalem; he is accompanied by his spoil and receives gifts as tribute. The ascent into *the high mount* now refers to Jesus' triumphal return to his heavenly glory when his work is completed (see also John 17: 4; Acts 1: 9). The *captives* are now the powers and forces opposed to God, which Jesus has defeated (see below on Col. 2: 15). Instead of receiving gifts as tribute from men, the conqueror distributes gifts among men.

9. The key words in the passage quoted are now drawn out. An 'ascent', the taking of higher rank and position, implies a 'descent', the holding of a lower rank. So Jesus claims supreme kingship over the world, not as an 'outside observer' but as one who has been involved in human life from the inside. He has shared in human life and in human death, and has come out of it victorious.

descended to the lowest level, down to the very earth would describe the distinctive Christian belief that Jesus, the Word of God, became man (compare John 1: 14, 'so the Word became flesh; he came to dwell among us...'). The alternative translation, given in the N.E.B. footnote, is to be preferred: 'descended to the regions beneath the earth'. This is a way of depicting physical death, and so stresses that Jesus also knows this experience and has surmounted it. For Jesus' invasion of the realm of the dead see also 1 Pet. 3: 19.

10. *ascended far above all heavens* means that Jesus proved victorious over all the forces that tried to crush both him and the cause of God that he represented. *heavens*: The Jews sometimes thought of God being separated from man by several heavens. Paul talks of being 'caught up as far as the third heaven' (2 Cor. 12: 2). This was the Jewish way of bringing out the majesty and glory of God. Here *heavens* may therefore denote the gap between God and man which Jesus has bridged by his successful mission, culminating in his *ascent* or triumphal return to God. *fill*, i.e. claim the universe as his own, as the power that ultimately matters.

11. The word *gifts* is now explained further. In order that the church may be keyed to its task of presenting Jesus and his importance to the world, certain people are given special qualities of leadership. The function of *apostles* and *prophets* has already been discussed (1: 1; 2: 20). A similar list of the leading ministers or officers in the Church is given in 1 Cor. 12: 28 ('Within our community God has appointed, in the first place apostles, in the second place prophets, thirdly teachers'). *evangelists*, i.e. those who preached the good news about Jesus. There seems to have been a definite office of evangelist in the early church, possessed by those who had a gift for this special work. Philip is described as an evangelist (Acts 21: 8). He was one of 'the Seven' mentioned in Acts 6: 1–6, prominent among whom was Stephen, the first Christian martyr. The Seven were appointed to see that the Church's money was properly distributed to those in need, but at least two of them, Stephen and Philip, also did the work of evangelists. The story of Philip suggests that such evangelists moved from place to place. *pastors* (Greek: 'shepherds') is a way of describing the leaders of a Christian congregation. They are probably the equivalent of 'the bishops' (Phil. 1: 1) and 'the elders' (e.g. Acts 20: 17). The local Jewish communities had elders who looked after their affairs; for example they formed a court of justice, and arranged the worship in the Jewish synagogues. It was most

natural that the early Christians should also use the office of elder, and we are told in Acts 14: 23 that Paul and Barnabas 'appointed elders for them in each congregation' i.e. in the newly founded churches of Galatia. *teachers* were holders of another office. They probably helped to give instruction to children and to those preparing for baptism, and were attached to each local church (Acts 13: 1, 'There were at Antioch, in the congregation there, certain prophets and teachers...'). Jesus had said, 'whoever wants to be first must be the willing slave of all' (Mark 10: 44), and had given a more exalted view of the purpose of leadership. So here the Church's ministers and leaders only exist to help the whole body of Christians to be true to its task of loyalty and witness to Jesus.

13. In the N.E.B. translation *faith* refers to Christian belief or doctrine. It could, however, be taken closely with *knowledge*, used in the sense of 'recognition' or 'acceptance'. Both words would then describe the Church's commitment to Jesus, *the Son of God*. Such commitment means recognition that Jesus is the point of *unity* where human life finds its full meaning. The Church has to attain to this unity, i.e. grow into all that it entails. *The full stature of Christ* or his perfection in his earthly life consisted in his unswerving belief that the cause of God would win the day, and in his unswerving obedience to God's will. This is the *mature manhood* demanded of Christians.

The Son of God is one of the earliest titles of Jesus. First and foremost, it describes his unique relationship to God and his unique place in God's plans. The term suggests the closeness to God of the person so described, and thus brings out the price paid by God in sending Jesus on his earthly mission. Jesus was commissioned at his baptism with the words, 'Thou art my Son, my Beloved; on thee my favour rests' (Mark 1: 11). The title is sometimes thought to depict Jesus as King; for at his coronation the Jewish king was addressed in a similar way (e.g. Ps. 2: 7, 'I will tell of the decree: The Lord said unto me, Thou art my son'). Others have connected the title with the description of the Jewish nation in Exodus 4: 22 ('Thus saith the Lord, Israel is my son, my firstborn'), in which case it would denote Jesus as the true representative of Israel. Among gentile Christians the term would suggest the divine status of Jesus. In any case Paul derives the title from the Christian tradition about Jesus, and we are told in Acts 9: 20 that Paul used it in his preaching in the immediate period after his conversion ('Soon he was proclaiming Jesus publicly in the synagogues: "This," he said, "is the Son of God" '). He also uses it in his earliest letters to express the special relationship between God and Jesus (e.g. Galatians 4: 4, 'God sent his own Son, born of a woman...'). In the Gospel of John, the full implications of Jesus' sonship are drawn out; it means that he is the Word of God (John 1: 1, 'When all things began, the Word already was. The Word dwelt with God and what God was, the Word was'). See also on Eph. 1: 3 and Col. 1: 15.

14. Paul and the early Christians were convinced that Jesus gave the key to life, and so the followers of Jesus are not to be at the mercy of every new-fangled philosophy and novel idea. It is tempting to think that behind a passage like this may have been Paul's visit to Athens and his experience of the people there, 'who had no time for anything but talking or hearing about the latest novelty' (Acts 17: 21). Paul lived in a world where there were many *crafty rogues* and *deceitful schemes*. He may have in mind the many false claimants to powers of magic and sorcery, who played upon people's credulity and made money by offering their services to ward off evil influences, to tell the future, and to give advice. Paul had on his journeys come across some of these *rogues* and showed them up for what they were. For example, there were the 'sorcerer', Bar-Jesus, that Paul met in Cyprus (Acts 13: 6), and the 'slave girl who was possessed by an oracular spirit and brought large profits to her owners by telling fortunes' (Acts 16: 16).

15. *let us speak the truth*, or rather 'let us keep to the

truth', i.e. the good news of God seen in Jesus Christ. *to grow up into Christ* means an ever deepening understanding of how he and all that he has made known to us of God apply to our situation and lives here and now.

16. Here (perhaps as in the similar passage, Col. 2: 18-19) the *body* is the Church, which, through the *gifts* mentioned in 4: 11, grows to be the effective instrument of God. But it can only do this if it is dependent on its *head*, i.e. its controlling power, Jesus, and if the spirit of Christian *love* informs its activities. The *body* here is looked at from the point of view of ancient medical science, according to which the body is held together (*a*) by the contact of one part with another and (*b*) by the *joints* (i.e. the nerves and tissues) which bind the different parts into one. All the parts have their function (their *due activity*) to perform.   *

THE CHRISTIAN REVOLUTION

This then is my word to you, and I urge it upon you in 17 the Lord's name. Give up living like pagans with their good-for-nothing notions. Their wits are beclouded, 18 they are strangers to the life that is in God, because ignorance prevails among them and their minds have grown hard as stone. Dead to all feeling, they have 19 abandoned themselves to vice, and stop at nothing to satisfy their foul desires. But that is not how you learned 20 Christ. For were you not told of him, were you not as 21 Christians taught the truth as it is in Jesus?—that, leaving 22 your former way of life, you must lay aside that old human nature which, deluded by its lusts, is sinking towards death. You must be made new in mind and 23 spirit, and put on the new nature of God's creating, 24 which shows itself in the just and devout life called for by the truth.

✻   Paul warns his hearers that the Christian way of life will cut across much that is accepted in the world or society around them. He is describing the general tone of the contemporary world, where, as in our own society, so much was based on self-interest.

17. *in the Lord's name*, i.e. on his authority. *pagans* (or 'Gentiles'): those who have no knowledge of the true God or of the standard of morality that he requires. *good-for-nothing notions* (Greek: 'in the vanity of their mind'). This language is used in the Old Testament in connection with the desertion of the true God, and the following of false gods (e.g. Jer. 2: 5, 'Thus saith the Lord, What unrighteousness have your fathers found in me, that they are gone far from me, and have walked after vanity and are become vain?').

18. *Their wits are beclouded* (Greek: 'they are darkened in mind'), i.e. they are out of touch with God's will. *the life that is in God*: it is only by being attuned to God and by giving obedience to him that the full potentialities of human nature can be achieved. *ignorance*, i.e. of the purpose of life. *their minds have grown hard as stone* is literally 'because of the hardness of their heart', a way of describing the refusal of human beings to recognize the voice of God (see e.g. 2 Chron. 36: 13, 'but he [King Zedekiah] hardened his heart from turning unto the Lord').

19. To be *dead to all feeling* is to be insensitive to the demands of God and the needs of one's fellow human beings. *vice* is the ruthless attitude, which must get its own ends at any cost. *foul desires* (Greek: 'every uncleanness') include not only sexual lusts, but all those desires that lead to low and unworthy conduct.

20. Those addressed had *learned Christ*, i.e. had been pupils in his school, where a very different lesson about life had been learnt. There may be some reference here to the teaching and training that these Christians had received before their baptism.

21. *told of him* (Greek: 'did you not hear him?'). They

had not listened to Jesus Christ speaking, but had heard of him as the central figure of the Gospel. *As Christians* (Greek 'in him'), i.e. as part of Jesus Christ's Church. *the truth,* that God is king claiming our allegiance, was taught and acted on by Jesus in his earthly life, and demonstrated in his death and resurrection.

22. To have learnt the lesson of Jesus Christ is to accept a revolution or change in one's life which can be compared to *laying aside* or disposing of old clothes and obtaining new ones. Later it was customary at baptism to discard one's old clothes, and put on new white robes on coming out of the water. *that old human nature* (Greek: 'the old man') stands for all that we have in common with Adam, who in the story of Gen. 3 represents the person who makes 'self' his god. *deluded by its lusts,* i.e. into thinking that self-satisfaction is what matters. Such an attitude means *death* because it defeats the end or purpose for which man exists.

23–24. One's whole attitude to living has to be given a new twist. This involves accepting the *new nature* or 'new character' which is portrayed in the human Jesus. The qualities that made up his life were selflessness, obedience to God, and love for people; he therefore displayed a character *of God's creating,* i.e. one which followed the pattern intended by God. Such a life is *just,* because it faces the demands of God, and devout, because it makes him the centre. It is also a life *called for by the truth,* i.e. the truth about God and the way of life that he demands, as revealed in Jesus.

The 'revolution' described here was vividly depicted in early Christian baptism when the candidate was immersed beneath the waters as a sign of death to the past, and came up from the water as the sign of a new life in company with Jesus. ✡

ADVICE FOR CHRISTIAN LIVING

25 Then throw off falsehood; speak the truth to each other, for all of us are the parts of one body.

26 If you are angry, do not let anger lead you into sin;
27 do not let sunset find you still nursing it; leave no loophole for the devil.

28 The thief must give up stealing, and instead work hard and honestly with his own hands, so that he may have something to share with the needy.

29 No bad language must pass your lips, but only what is good and helpful to the occasion, so that it brings a
30 blessing to those who hear it. And do not grieve the Holy Spirit of God, for that Spirit is the seal with which you were marked for the day of our final liberation.
31 Have done with spite and passion, all angry shouting and cursing, and bad feeling of every kind.

32 Be generous to one another, tender-hearted, forgiving one another as God in Christ forgave you.

5 In a word, as God's dear children, try to be like him,
2 and live in love as Christ loved you, and gave himself up on your behalf as an offering and sacrifice whose fragrance is pleasing to God.

✻ Some detailed advice for living the Christian life now follows, together with some characteristics of the 'new nature'. For this section see also Col. 3: 8–14.

25. See Zechariah 8: 16, 'Speak the truth to one another'. *throw off* is thought to have been a set formula used in the moral teaching of the early church; here it looks back to 4: 22 ('lay aside'). *speak the truth* means the avoidance of all underhand and deceitful dealings with fellow human beings. The basis of this command is that we *are the parts of one*

body, i.e. we 'belong together' as members of the one community, the Church (see also 4: 4).

26–27. There is a righteous *anger*, which can be the result e.g. of strong feeling about injustice, but normally anger is irritation with other people. If it is harboured, it can lead to embitterment and hatred, and so play into the hands of *the devil*, the forces at work against God. *do not let sunset find you* is another way of saying, 'do not harbour resentment but cut short the chain of evil quickly'. For Jesus' teaching on the seriousness of anger see Matthew 5: 22, 'But what I tell you is this: Anyone who nurses anger against his brother must be brought to judgement.'

28. The Christian attitude to earning one's livelihood is 'an honest day's work for an honest day's pay'. *stealing* here includes 'get rich quick' schemes, which can cheat and defraud other people. There is also the duty of helping *the needy* or less fortunate with one's money.

29. *bad* or 'rancid', i.e. language that 'cuts' or hurts other people, and causes mischief. The Christian uses his tongue in a constructive way. Jesus had said, 'I tell you this: there is not a thoughtless word that comes from men's lips but they will have to account for it on the day of judgement' (Matt. 12: 36). The Letter of James also has something instructive to say about the dangers of the tongue, e.g. 3: 7, 'Beasts and birds of every kind, creatures that crawl on the ground or swim in the sea, can be subdued and have been subdued by mankind; but no man can subdue the tongue. It is an intractable evil, charged with deadly venom.'

30. To be disloyal is for the Christian not merely disobedience to a law, but a personal affront to God's *Holy Spirit* who claims us as his sphere of influence and is wronged by rival claims to our loyalty. The experience of the Holy Spirit or God's power here and now is the *seal* or guarantee of the Christian's hope (see also 1: 13). This hope is that of being released from everything that prevents full union with God. The *final liberation* is here connected with the *day* of

Jesus Christ, when God becomes all in all, and Christians 'shall always be with the Lord' (1 Thess. 4: 17).

31. *spite* could be translated 'bitterness'. The list of vices continues in the Greek as follows: 'passion and anger and shouting and cursing...' We thus pass from the feeling of embitterment to its outward expression in *shouting* or active quarrelling, and in *cursing*, i.e. the use of abusive language.

This for the moment concludes the negative teaching on vices that are to be avoided. The positive characteristics of the Christian life are now stated.

32. Jesus himself taught the need for a *generous* love and compassion, independent of expected return (Matt. 5: 46, 'If you love only those who love you, what reward can you expect?'). Jesus also showed this love in his life. Such love includes a willingness to forgive, i.e. to accept people back as though nothing had happened to break the relationship between us and them. But what inspires us to do this is the picture of God who *in Christ forgave*, i.e. took us back to himself.

5: 1–2. *God's dear children*, i.e. those who are restored to his family circle, have to show the qualities found in him who is the head of the family. These qualities include especially *love*, which has been brought very close to us in the self-giving love of Jesus, seen in his life and death. Jesus' perfect obedience to God, even when it meant death, is here described in the language of animal sacrifices and other offerings which were thought to be demanded by God and acceptable to him.

whose fragrance is pleasing is literally 'for a sweet-smelling odour'. This term at a less advanced stage in the Jewish religion had described the 'sweet savour' of the sacrificed animal, which God was supposed actually to smell. With a more exalted idea of God, the phrase became a vivid way of saying that the sacrifice was pleasing to God (e.g. Exod. 29: 18, 'And thou shalt burn the whole ram upon the altar: it is a burnt offering unto the Lord: it is a sweet savour, an offering made by fire unto the Lord').

We may also note two further points:

(*a*) Jesus himself taught that his followers were to be like God in the sense described here (e.g. Matt. 5: 44–45, 'Love your enemies and pray for your persecutors; only so can you be children of your heavenly Father, who makes his sun rise on good and bad alike, and sends the rain on the honest and the dishonest').

(*b*) The self-giving of Jesus is pictured in the language of animal sacrifice. The latter was seen by the early Christians to be an unworthy substitute for the perfect sacrifice, which was the offering of a life of obedience to God. This perfect sacrifice had been made by Jesus, and so animal sacrifice was obsolete and outmoded. For example, the writer of the Letter to the Hebrews argues that Jesus is the one who can say 'I have come, O God, to do thy will', and therefore the animal sacrifices prescribed under the Jewish law are superseded (Heb. 10: 5–10). *

THINGS TO AVOID

Fornication and indecency of any kind, or ruthless greed, 3 must not be so much as mentioned among you, as befits the people of God. No coarse, stupid, or flippant talk; 4 these things are out of place; you should rather be thanking God. For be very sure of this: no one given to 5 fornication or indecency, or the greed which makes an idol of gain, has any share in the kingdom of Christ and of God.

* A warning is given about the wrong use of sex and of the tongue, and about the dangers of greed. Verses 3 and 4 are constructed on similar lines. In verse 3 three vices are mentioned, followed by the grounds for avoiding them; in verse 4 the same pattern is followed. See also Col. 3: 5–8.

3. *fornication* covers the selfish and wrong use of sex, e.g.

outside the marriage bond. *indecency* includes the abuse of the sexual instinct, but can also refer to all that offends against God's moral law. Paul is dealing with people who had been brought up to treat sex in a free and easy fashion. *ruthless greed* was a desire to obtain as much as one could at the expense of others. This attitude was also thought to be among the worst evils by other writers and thinkers of this period. Below, in verse 5, it is seen as like the worship of a false god.

not mentioned. To talk about something can rouse an interest in it. The *people of God* (see above on 1: 1) always have the honour of Jesus to uphold. *coarse, stupid, or flippant talk* is in the Greek 'filthiness, silly talk, or coarse jesting'.

4. Again the reminder is given that we influence other people very much by our talk, e.g. 'dirty jokes' only add to the unhealthiness of people's minds. The tongue is much better employed in *thanking God.* If *thanking God* holds the centre of the stage, then in gratitude to God we try to live a life worthy of him.

5. *the kingdom of Christ and of God.* The Jews looked forward to the time when God would make a demonstration that he was King in his world, and would establish his kingdom. It was the claim of Jesus that in himself and his mission God was making this demonstration, and summoning men to own him as King (e.g. Mark 1: 14, 'Jesus came into Galilee proclaiming the Gospel of God: "The time has come; the kingdom of God is upon you"'). Christians are those who have entered God's kingdom; but the conduct mentioned here would disqualify one for citizenship in this kingdom. *greed* is an *idol*, because it is a worship of the false god, self. ✳

THE LIGHT OF THE WORLD

6 Let no one deceive you with shallow arguments; it is for all these things that God's dreadful judgement is
7 coming upon his rebel subjects. Have no part or lot

with them. For though you were once all darkness, now 8
as Christians you are light. Live like men who are at
home in daylight, for where light is, there all goodness 9
springs up, all justice and truth. Make sure what would 10
have the Lord's approval; take no part in the barren 11
deeds of darkness, but show them up for what they are.
The things they do in secret it would be shameful even 12
to mention. But everything, when once the light has 13
shown it up, is illumined, and everything thus illumined
is all light. And so the hymn says: 14

> 'Awake, sleeper,
> Rise from the dead,
> And Christ will shine upon you.'

* Much of this section is based on Jesus' saying: 'You are
light for all the world' (Matt. 5: 14).

6. *arguments*, i.e. in favour of living for self, are *shallow*
(Greek: 'vain') because they do not allow for God. *dreadful
judgement* stresses that human beings are accountable to God
and that those who disobey him will be brought to see the
error of their ways (see above on 2: 3).

7–8. *them*: either the *rebel subjects* or the vices just mentioned. *darkness*, suggestive of evil and badness, meant for
the Jews being out of touch with the will and purpose of God
and being in the power of forces opposed to him. *light*,
however, described God, and Christians are *light*, because
they belong to Jesus who is 'the light of the world' (John
8: 12), confronting the world with God's nature and purposes.
But Christians are to show themselves *at home in daylight* by
taking God's demands and purposes seriously. The same
thought is found in 1 John 2: 9 ('A man may say, "I am in
the light"; but if he hates his brother, he is still in the dark.
Only the man who loves his brother dwells in light').

9. *light* in the ordinary sense causes organic life to grow,

so the light of Jesus should bring to life in people the qualities mentioned: *goodness* (the doing of God's will), *justice* (fair treatment of others) and *truth* (straightforward dealing).

10. The Christian life is a continuous assessment: one asks, what is the viewpoint of Jesus on my situation?

11. There is not only the negative duty of refusing to be caught up in the low standards of the world around. Christians have also a positive one. Just as light lights up dark corners and reveals the dust, so Christians are *to show up* the evil and false ideals around them. This is done by the example of their lives and by a refusal to conform to the standards of others as well as by vocal protest.

12. Much that goes on *in secret*, i.e. under the surface of a society that seems very respectable, is often disreputable. Paul fears that the *mention* of some of these practices would only spread their evil influence, and play on people's interest in what is sordid and scandalous. The best antidote to these practices will be the clear stand made by Christians on behalf of the way of life approved by God.

13–14. Where there is darkness, there is need of light to illuminate the scene. Where is this light to be found? The answer is given in the quotation which follows. It is not taken from the Old Testament but probably comes from a Christian hymn, used at baptism. It was most likely addressed to the candidate for baptism, who has been a *sleeper* and one of the *dead* in the sense of being indifferent to the things of God. He is now summoned to rise to a new life centred on God, and receives the light of Jesus to show him how to live. This in turn makes him into a beacon, exposing the shallowness of much that is around him. The hymn would appropriately be said at the point when the candidate came up from the water after his immersion. For baptism as 'enlightenment' see also Heb. 6: 4.   *

RIGHT USE OF THE PRESENT

Be most careful then how you conduct yourselves: like 15
sensible men, not like simpletons. Use the present 16
opportunity to the full, for these are evil days. So do 17
not be fools, but try to understand what the will of the
Lord is. Do not give way to drunkenness and the dissipa- 18
tion that goes with it, but let the Holy Spirit fill you:
speak to one another in psalms, hymns, and songs; sing 19
and make music in your hearts to the Lord; and in the 20
name of our Lord Jesus Christ give thanks every day
for everything to our God and Father.

Be subject to one another out of reverence for Christ. 21

* Paul now discusses the right approach to situations that
are difficult and unpromising. He also points to the right
source of Christian joy.

15. If Christians are centres of light, then they must
show good common sense in living up to this privilege.

16. *use* (Greek: 'purchase' or 'buy up'): a word connected with reckoning up what one can buy. *evil days*: times
when people are hostile or indifferent to the Gospel. Such a
situation is not to be faced with apathy, but constructively,
using every chance of witnessing to Jesus. The *fools'* way
would be to sit back and do nothing with a kind of pious
resignation. The sensible and positive way is to see how the
situation can be used for God (*what the will of the Lord is*).

18. The Christian is not to escape into a world of artificial
gaiety by *drunkenness*, i.e. over-drinking alcohol, or, as we
might add today, by taking drugs of various kinds. The
right kind of intoxication and joy is that inspired by the
Holy Spirit, the power of God at work in Christians to make
them feel near to him.

19. This joy will be outwardly expressed in the meetings

of the Christian fellowship for worship. *psalms* from the Old Testament probably had a place in Christian worship from the earliest times. *hymns* and *songs* were probably mainly Christian compositions, and may well have included some of the songs preserved in Revelation (e.g. 5: 9–10), as well as the 'Song of Mary' (Luke 1: 46) and the 'Song of Simeon' (Luke 2: 29). *in your hearts*: this music is to be the outward sign of a deeply felt thanksgiving.

20. *in the name of*, i.e. as the representatives of Jesus in whom God's mercies are revealed.

21. This means a willingness to respect and honour the wishes and needs of others. *reverence for Christ*, because such an attitude forms part of the love that he taught and lived.   ✲

THE DUTIES OF WIVES

22, 23 Wives, be subject to your husbands as to the Lord; for the man is the head of the woman, just as Christ also is the head of the church. Christ is, indeed, the Saviour
24 of the body; but just as the church is subject to Christ, so must women be to their husbands in everything.

✲ This section and the ones that follow show how Jesus and his message have a bearing on the relationship between various classes of people. A similar scheme of instruction is found in Col. 3: 18 — 4: 1 and 1 Pet. 2: 13 — 3: 7. It may be based on a 'church catechism' or manual of instruction which was used in the preparation of candidates for baptism, and which set out the duties of Christians. Such a catechism may be referred to in Rom. 6: 17 ('But God be thanked, you, who once were slaves of sin, have yielded whole-hearted obedience to the pattern of teaching to which you were made subject'), and in 1 Thess. 4: 1 ('We passed on to you the tradition of the way we must live to please God'). The Stoics, whose leading beliefs have already been discussed on

p. 20, had developed a moral code dealing with human relationships. For example, a prominent Stoic of the time was the Roman author and politician Seneca, who was an adviser of the Emperor Nero (A.D. 54-68), and a contemporary of Paul, and also a brother of Gallio, the 'governor' of Achaia (Acts 18: 12). He speaks of 'that part of philosophy which gives advice suitable to each individual person, without its applying to everyone, but advises the husband how to behave towards his wife, the father how he is to bring up his children, the master how he is to control his slaves' (Letter 94: 1).

It was natural that the early Christians should also develop their own codes of this kind, especially as the teaching and life of Jesus had given new insight into human relationships.

22. In instructing wives to *be subject* to their husbands, Paul started with the social order as he knew it, where the husband had absolute authority over his household and everyone in it, including his wife. But Paul puts a different complexion on the picture when he sees the husband's authority over his wife as modelled on that claimed by Jesus over his church (*as to the Lord*). For it is stressed in 5: 25-33 below that the relationship of Jesus to his church is one of love. Therefore the husband's authority over his wife does not take the form of tyranny over his wife, but is permeated all through with love.

23. Paul had already argued that *the man is the head of the woman*, i.e. is senior to her and has authority over her, in his dealings with the Corinthian Church (1 Cor. 11: 2-16). He probably takes this strong line because he is nervous lest some of the claims being made by the women at Corinth will, if granted, increase the disorder in the congregation there.

Whether similar fears underlie the present passage, it is impossible to say. But there is every indication that Paul understood the difference that Jesus had made to the status of women (e.g. Gal. 3: 28, 'There is no such thing as Jew and Greek, slave and freeman, male and female; for you are all one person in Christ Jesus'). There are also signs that Paul saw that in marriage husband and wife are equal partners who complement each other (e.g. 1 Cor. 11: 11, 'And yet in Christ's fellowship woman is as essential to man as man to woman').

Christ is *the head of the church* in several senses. First, he is the Church's founder. It was his appearance, alive from the dead, that assured his disciples that he was undefeated and transformed them into a community committed to his cause and service. Secondly, he is the Church's *head* in the sense that he is the driving force behind the Church's life and work. Thirdly, he is the *head* in that he claims complete loyalty and obedience from his Church.

24. *the body* is another way of talking of the Church. *Saviour of the body* indicates further the sense in which Jesus can claim to be head of the Church. He is the one who has saved or delivered Christians from false ideas about the meaning of life, and has pioneered the way to union with the true God.

Saviour is a title of Jesus probably in use from an early period of the church (Acts 13: 23, '...God, as he promised, has brought Israel a saviour, Jesus'). It is used of God in both the Old and New Testaments (e.g. Luke 1: 47 '...rejoice, my spirit, in God my saviour'). In the time of Paul it could describe various kinds of benefactors. The Roman emperors were called 'Saviour', as having brought peace to the world. The gods of the Mystery cults (already mentioned) were also given the title. When applied to Jesus, it marks him out as the true and lasting benefactor of mankind.

but is a literal translation of the Greek word used; a better rendering would be 'so then'. If the parallel between the Church and the wife is perfectly drawn, then the woman must be subject *in everything* to the husband, as Jesus demands from the Church a complete submission to his authority. But this is tempered by the demand placed on the husband in verses 25 ff.   *

THE DUTIES OF HUSBANDS

Husbands, love your wives, as Christ also loved the 25
church and gave himself up for it, to consecrate it, 26
cleansing it by water and word, so that he might present 27
the church to himself all glorious, with no stain or
wrinkle or anything of the sort, but holy and without
blemish. In the same way men also are bound to love 28
their wives, as they love their own bodies. In loving his
wife a man loves himself. For no one ever hated his own 29
body: on the contrary, he provides and cares for it; and
that is how Christ treats the church, because it is his 30
body, of which we are living parts. Thus it is that (in the 31
words of Scripture) 'a man shall leave his father and
mother and shall be joined to his wife, and the two shall
become a single body'. It is a great truth that is hidden 32
here. I for my part refer it to Christ and to the church,
but it applies also individually: each of you must love 33
his wife as his very self; and the woman must see to it
that she pays her husband all respect.

* The relationship between husband and wife is now
further discussed. The husband's attitude to his wife is seen
to be modelled on that of Jesus towards his Church.

25. The husband's *love* is to be based on the pattern of the
self-giving love of Jesus, which he showed in becoming man,
in serving human beings in his earthly life, and in dying for
them.

26. The aim of Jesus' love is now described in language
taken from baptism. Terms applied normally in the New
Testament to the baptism of individuals are here used of the
Church as a whole. For the language we may compare 1 Cor.
6: 11, 'But you have been through the purifying waters;

you have been dedicated to God…' Jesus' purpose is to *consecrate* the Church, i.e. to make it a perfect reflection of his mind and purpose. This involved *cleansing it*, i.e. wiping away its sins through the assurance of God's forgiveness, and giving a new start. Such *cleansing* is portrayed in the rite of baptism, which is marked by two important features: (*a*) the use of *water*, in which the candidate is immersed, and (*b*) the *word*, the candidate's open confession of his faith that 'Jesus is Lord'.

27. With the translation *present the church to himself* the picture is perhaps that of Jesus the king receiving acceptable people into his court. But it is equally possible to translate: 'make the church for himself all glorious'. The Church is to be *glorious* or 'bright with God's glory', i.e. it is to be a centre of light reflecting God's will and purpose. *stain* (or 'spot') and *wrinkle* are ways of talking about disfigurement. *holy* means 'set apart', i.e. given over to the service of Jesus. *without blemish* is a term taken from the language of animal sacrifices; it described the perfection required in the animal victim (e.g. Exod. 12: 5, 'Your lamb shall be without blemish'). Here it is used of the perfect obedience required of Christians.

28–29. The appeal to husbands to love their wives has so far been based on the love of Jesus for his Church. Now a further reason is given, based on the idea of self-love. Men *love their own bodies*, i.e. they have a deep-rooted instinct to protect and care for themselves. *In loving his wife a man loves himself*, because she is part of himself, not only through the union of love in the sexual act, but also through the life-long partnership entered on together.

30. The appeal to the example of Jesus and the Church is now resumed. It has been said that the husband ought to love his wife as part of himself. The pattern for this conduct can be found in the relationship between Jesus and his Church. *Christ treats the church* with loving care *because it is his body*, of which we are living parts or, more literally translated, 'because

we are the limbs of his body'. In his earlier letters Paul thinks of Jesus as the body or organism to which his followers belong as the living parts (e.g. 1 Cor. 12: 12, 'For Christ is like a single body with its many limbs and organs, which, many as they are, together make up one body'). Paul now returns to this picture to underline that the Church is part of the very being of the risen Jesus, and as such cared for and loved.

31. Paul has been talking of the close union between (a) husband and wife and (b) Jesus and his Church. This close union is now illustrated by a quotation from the Old Testament which carried weight and authority with Paul and the early Christians as pointing forward to the coming of Jesus and showing the need for his mission. The passage is taken from Gen. 2: 24, where the writer uses the story of how God made woman out of a man to show the basic unity of man and woman.

32-33. *It is a great truth that is hidden here* is literally 'this secret is important'. 'secret' means (as the N.E.B. makes clear) a hidden revelation of God contained in the words of scripture. Paul had already described the Old Testament as 'a kind of tutor in charge of us until Christ should come' (Gal. 3: 24), and therefore he and other early Christians read it in the light of their knowledge of Jesus and saw all kinds of hidden references to him in the text. So here the passage from Genesis speaks of something deeper than appears on the surface; it refers *to Christ and to the church* i.e. to the binding union between the two.

But the literal meaning of the passage is not to be neglected; *it applies individually*, i.e. it has something of relevance to the individual husband and wife. It shows that the wife is part of the husband's *very self*, and so underlines the statement of verse 28 that in loving his wife a man loves himself. The passage concludes with a return to the husband's authority and position as head of the household; as such the husband will deserve *all respect* from his wife.

A parallel is drawn here between husband and wife on the one hand, and Jesus and the Church on the other. This brings to mind the Old Testament picture of God as the husband or bridegroom, and the Jewish nation as his wife or bride (Isa. 62: 5, 'and as the bridegroom rejoiceth over the bride, so shall thy God rejoice over thee'). There are other passages in the New Testament where Jesus is likened to a husband, and the church to a bride (e.g. 2 Cor. 11: 2, 'I betrothed you to Christ, thinking to present you as a chaste virgin to her true and only husband'). The idea of Jesus as the bridegroom may have been suggested by words of Jesus himself (Mark 2: 19, 'Jesus said to them, "Can you expect the bridegroom's friends to fast while the bridegroom is with them? As long as the bridegroom is with them, there can be no fasting" '). ✻

ADVICE TO CHILDREN AND FATHERS

6 Children, obey your parents, for it is right that you
2 should. 'Honour your father and mother' is the first
3 commandment with a promise attached, in the words: 'that it may be well with you and that you may live long in the land'.

4 You fathers, again, must not goad your children to resentment, but give them the instruction, and the correction, which belong to a Christian upbringing.

✻ The section implies that children may have been in the congregation when the 'manifesto' was read.

1. respect of children for their parents is to form the basis of family life.

2. The Ten Commandments are still important for Christians. For the fifth, quoted here, see Exod. 20: 12 and Deut. 5: 16.

3. The *promise* relates to the land of Canaan which the

Israelites are about to inherit. It is now a far better heritage that is involved (see above on 1:11). A healthy family life is seen to be part of God's purposes.

4. Parents are to be understanding; while discipline is good, it must not cause *resentment*, i.e. give the impression that children cannot do anything right. What matters is that the children should be helped to understand the significance of Jesus. Correction has the positive aim of developing qualities worthy of him. The Jews were supposed to instruct their children in what God had done for their nation (e.g. Exod. 12: 26, 'And it shall come to pass, when your children shall say unto you, What mean ye by this service? that ye shall say, It is the sacrifice of the Lord's passover, who passed over the houses of the children of Israel in Egypt, when he smote the Egyptians and delivered our houses'). It is natural that parents who believe their faith to be valuable should present it to their children, just as they pass on their experience of life in other fields. ✳

ADVICE TO SLAVES AND MASTERS

Slaves, obey your earthly masters with fear and trem- 5
bling, single-mindedly, as serving Christ. Do not offer 6
merely the outward show of service, to curry favour
with men, but, as slaves of Christ, do whole-heartedly
the will of God. Give the cheerful service of those who 7
serve the Lord, not men. For you know that whatever 8
good each man may do, slave or free, will be repaid
him by the Lord.

You masters, also, must do the same by them. Give up 9
using threats; remember you both have the same Master
in heaven, and he has no favourites.

✳ The institution of slavery was part of the social and economic system of the ancient world. The slave might be employed

in industry, in administration, and in private households. He was technically the possession of the person whom he served, but often received good treatment. There was probably a fairly strong element of slaves in the early Church. In society, slave and freeman are classes apart, but in the Church the position is altered, because people are there accounted important not by reason of class, but by reason of the fact that everyone is loved and wanted by Jesus (Col. 3: 11, 'There is no question here of Greek and Jew... freeman, slave; but Christ is all, and is in all'). But this does not mean that slaves are to be released from their slavery (see below, p. 181), to 'get beyond themselves' and to neglect their duties. Why did not the early Church attack the existence of slavery? It was the function of the Church at that time to bring to people the good news of the Gospel, and its impact on human relationships. To have sought to create an economic and social upheaval would not have served this end. There was also a firm expectation that the present world order would soon end (e.g. 1 Cor. 7: 31, 'For the whole frame of this world is passing away'). This expectation perhaps prevented the early Christians from making any attack on slavery as an institution, though this factor might easily be exaggerated. The spread of the Gospel would create a climate of opinion in which the social order would be reviewed and reformed, however dimly the early Christians discerned that this would happen. On slavery see also below, p. 179.

5. *earthly*, as opposed to their heavenly Lord, Jesus. Their *fear* and *trembling* are to arise from seeing themselves as performing a service for Jesus in doing their work well. *single-mindedly*, i.e. showing the same wholehearted devotion as they would to Jesus Christ.

6–7. The slaves are to be conscientious, because it is *the will of God*, and because they, like other Christians, are *slaves of Christ*, i.e. under his control, and so expected to give of their best. The same motive must lie behind their *cheerful service*, which was considered to be a virtue in slaves. A papyrus found in Egypt and dating to a time a little later than Ephesians gives us the last will and testament of someone who bequeathes to his slaves their freedom in recognition of their 'cheerful service and firm affection'.

8. Jesus himself promised reward to his faithful followers (e.g. Matt. 5: 12, 'accept it with gladness and exultation, for you have a rich reward in heaven'). People need to be assured that a particular way of life has a future in it and leads somewhere. Here the repayment may be the approval of Jesus in the day of judgement (see 2 Cor. 5: 10, 'For we must all have our lives laid open before the tribunal of Christ, where each must receive what is due to him for his conduct in the body, good or bad').

9. Similarly, Christian masters are not 'laws to themselves' in their treatment of their slaves. They are responsible for their conduct to the Lord Jesus. Their relationship with their slaves will therefore be based on Christian love, and not on *threats* of punishment. The master cannot claim superiority to his slave, as they are both under the orders of the Lord Jesus who *has no favourites*. This is an important characteristic of God in the Old Testament (e.g. 2 Chron. 19: 7, 'for there is no iniquity with the Lord our God, nor respect of persons, nor taking of gifts'). It is striking how easily the early Christians applied to Jesus terms that originally applied to God. Advice to treat slaves well is also found in writers contemporary with Paul. For example, Seneca, the Roman philosopher and politician, already mentioned on p. 83, says that slaves are not to be treated merely as pieces of property. ✵

THE CHRISTIAN WARFARE WITH EVIL

Finally then, find your strength in the Lord, in his 10 mighty power. Put on all the armour which God 11 provides, so that you may be able to stand firm against

12 the devices of the devil. For our fight is not against human foes, but against cosmic powers, against the authorities and potentates of this dark world, against the

13 superhuman forces of evil in the heavens. Therefore, take up God's armour; then you will be able to stand your ground when things are at their worst, to complete

14 every task and still to stand. Stand firm, I say. Buckle on the belt of truth; for coat of mail put on integrity;

15 let the shoes on your feet be the gospel of peace, to give

16 you firm footing; and, with all these, take up the great shield of faith, with which you will be able to quench

17 all the flaming arrows of the evil one. Take salvation for helmet; for sword, take that which the Spirit gives you

18 —the words that come from God. Give yourselves wholly to prayer and entreaty; pray on every occasion in the power of the Spirit. To this end keep watch and

19 persevere, always interceding for all God's people; and pray for me, that I may be granted the right words when I open my mouth, and may boldly and freely make known his hidden purpose, for which I am an ambassador

20 —in chains. Pray that I may speak of it boldly, as it is my duty to speak.

* There are forces at work in the world opposed to God and his purposes. The mission of Jesus is the scene of a conflict between God and the forces of evil. In this conflict Jesus is victorious, and so assures us that God is King and will achieve his purposes. The present section makes the point that those who belong to Jesus are of necessity involved in the same struggle; they are to be God's centre of resistance against evil. The background to the language of 'warfare' used here may be noted:

(*a*) In Paul's time philosophers described human life as a

warfare, and the follower of a particular cult or sect might be called a 'soldier'.

(*b*) Ancient Babylonian stories describe in terms of warfare the conflict between the god Marduk and the powers of chaos. This language is then used by Jewish writers to depict God's fight with unrighteousness and wrong social dealing. We should compare with our present section Isa. 59: 17 ('He [God], put on righteousness as a breastplate, and a helmet of salvation upon his head; he put on garments of vengeance for clothing, and wrapped himself in fury as a mantle' R.S.V.) and Wisd. of Sol. 5: 17–20 ('The Lord will take his zeal as his whole armour, and will arm all creation to repel his enemies; he will put on righteousness as a breastplate, and wear impartial justice as a helmet; he will take holiness as an invincible shield, and sharpen stern wrath for a sword...' R.S.V.).

(*c*) The Jewish sect at Qumran (mentioned on p. 59) believed that there would be a great conflict between themselves, as the representatives of God, and the forces of evil. This is depicted in the so-called 'War Rule', 'on the day of calamity, the sons of light shall battle with the company of darkness amid the shouts of a mighty multitude...' (*The Dead Sea Scrolls in English*, G. Vermes, Penguin Books, p. 125). The language used to describe this conflict is couched in military terms taken from the art of war as practised by the Romans.

10. Self-reliance is out of the question. Evil can only be fought with the aid of the *power* of Jesus, demonstrated in his resurrection, i.e. in his triumph over the forces of evil opposed to him.

11. *all the armour* (Greek: 'panoply') was the full range of armour used by the Roman soldier in a life-and-death struggle. *stand firm* means to maintain one's position in the line of battle. The *devil*, i.e. the forces opposed to God, uses all sorts of *devices* or tricks, like earthly enemies. Evil can, for example, be made to look attractive and pleasant (2 Cor. 11: 14, 'Satan himself masquerades as an angel of light').

12. *against cosmic powers, against the authorities.* These terms have already been mentioned in 1: 20 ('all government and authority') and 3: 10 ('the rulers and authorities'). They were seen there to represent superhuman powers of evil that are rivalling God for the control of his world. They are also referred to in *potentates of this dark world* (Greek: 'the world-rulers of this darkness'), and in *the superhuman forces of evil*. The world was thought to be *dark* because human beings refuse to face the claims of the true God, and are under the control of evil forces. *in the heavens* stresses that these powers are competing with God. For us they represent the control exercised over human minds by false ideals, various kinds of prejudices and bad influences, and the setting up of the false god of 'self'. To fight such deeply entrenched forces can be harder than combating *human foes*.

13. *take up* is the regular word for equipping oneself with weapons. *when things are at their worst* (Greek: 'in the evil day'), i.e. when the enemy's pressure is hottest. *complete every task* means 'to meet every challenge'. *stand*, i.e. with formation unbroken.

14. Round the waist the Roman soldier wore *the belt* ('slacken your belts' was the equivalent of our command 'stand easy'). *truth*: the knowledge of God's nature and his plan for human life, revealed in Jesus, with which the Christian must encircle himself as with a belt.

15. *coat of mail*, or 'breastplate'. *integrity* (Greek: 'righteousness') might refer to the Christian's living up to conduct worthy of God. More likely it describes God's rescue operation in Jesus Christ, bringing the assurance that the Christian is right with God. *let the shoes...footing* may also be translated 'having put on the gospel of peace as military boots by way of preparation'. Ironically it is God's peace-making activity in reconciling us to himself that helps us to take a firm stand in the warfare with evil.

16. *with all these*, or 'above all'. *the great shield* was a large quadrangular shield devised to catch and extinguish ignited

arrows. *the evil one*, i.e. the devil: the sum total of the forces arrayed against God. *faith* is confidence in the rightness and final victory of God's cause.

17. The *helmet* is another piece of protective armour. *salvation* is God's rescue operation effected in Jesus Christ. This brings home to us God's love and the assurance that God will triumph over the forces opposed to him. The *sword* is the weapon of assault. *the words that come from God* (Greek: ' the word of God ') include all the teaching that God has given about himself. For Paul this would include the Old Testament, and all that God had made known of himself in the teaching and mission of Jesus. All this is a weapon that *the Spirit gives*, i.e. God's Holy Spirit can help and guide us to use it rightly.

18. *prayer*, the laying of our needs before God, is also part of the Christian armour. Perhaps Paul has particularly in mind prayer for the achievement of God's purposes. *in the power of the Spirit*, i.e. asking for the guidance of God's Holy Spirit to pray for the right things. *keep watch* and *persevere* are apt commands for a soldier at his post. Intercession, or prayer for other people, is one of the ways in which we co-operate with God (2 Cor. 1: 11, 'Yes, he will continue to deliver us, if you will co-operate by praying for us').

19–20. The power to say *the right words* at the right time in conveying the Gospel is something God-given. *ambassador* describes Paul as the representative of Jesus. *in chains*: an unusual condition for an envoy, who would have diplomatic immunity. But Paul sees his *chains*, i.e. his imprisonment, as an advertisement for the claims of Jesus (see also Phil. 1: 13, 'My imprisonment in Christ's cause has become common knowledge to all at headquarters here, and indeed among the public at large'). Paul knows that the prayers of other Christians are an important way in which they can co-operate with him. *

CLOSING REMARKS AND FINAL GREETING

21   You will want to know about my affairs, and how I am; Tychicus will give you all the news. He is our dear
22 brother and trustworthy helper in the Lord's work. I am sending him to you on purpose to let you know all about us, and to put fresh heart into you.

23   Peace to the brotherhood and love, with faith, from God
24 the Father and the Lord Jesus Christ. God's grace be with all who love our Lord Jesus Christ, grace and immortality.

✴ 21. For Tychicus see above p. 18. This commendation of him is similar to the one in Col. 4: 7–9. As we saw above (p. 19), Ephesians may be a manifesto composed by Tychicus on authority from Paul. He would naturally repeat from Colossians the nature of the mission that he has been given by Paul. *brother* is an affectionate term for a 'fellow Christian'. *helper* (Greek: 'deacon') does not refer to an actual office held, but to one who is helping forward the cause of Jesus (see also above on 3: 7).

22. *all about us*, i.e. what is happening to Paul in Rome.

23. The concluding greeting in letters of Paul's time was usually 'fare you well'—an expression of good wishes. As, however, with the opening greeting, so here, Paul introduces Christian language. The final greeting in our present letter is slightly longer than in most of Paul's other letters (e.g. Gal. 6: 18, 'The grace of our Lord Jesus Christ be with your spirit, my brothers. Amen'). It is in effect a prayer that the Christians addressed may share in all the benefits that come from God's *peace* and *love*, i.e. God's restoration of human beings to himself, and his generous love seen in the life and death of Jesus. This peace and love should call out *faith*, i.e. confident trust in God. *God the Father and the Lord Jesus Christ* occurs in both the opening and closing greetings of this letter (see on 1: 2–3).

24. *grace* often features in the closing greetings of Paul's letters. *those who love our Lord,* i.e. those who obey him and put him first in response to his love shown to human beings. *and immortality* (Greek: 'with immortality') can be taken in several ways:

(*a*) it could go closely with *grace,* i.e. a full response to God's favour seen in Jesus will result in *immortality;*

(*b*) it could be taken with love, i.e., this is a love that results in *immortality.*

(*b*) is perhaps preferable and more natural. This living relationship of love with the risen Jesus has a lasting quality about it and is something that can survive all obstacles. This is well expressed in Rom. 8: 38-39, 'For I am convinced that there is nothing in death or life, in the realm of spirits or superhuman powers, in the world as it is, or the world as it shall be, in the forces of the universe, in heights or depths— nothing in all creation that can separate us from the love of God in Christ Jesus our Lord.' It is a relationship, too, that results in the full life awaiting Christians, when God has completed his purposes and is all in all (1 Cor. 15: 51, 'Listen! I will unfold a mystery: we shall not all die, but we shall all be changed in a flash, in the twinkling of an eye, at the last trumpet-call. For the trumpet will sound, and the dead will rise immortal, and we shall be changed. This perishable being must be clothed with the imperishable, and what is mortal must be clothed with immortality'). It is appropriate that Ephesians ends on the note of immortality, the quest of so many in Paul's day.

✽   ✽   ✽   ✽   ✽   ✽   ✽   ✽   ✽   ✽   ✽   ✽   ✽

THE CHALLENGE OF EPHESIANS FOR TODAY

(1) *The Rallying Point*

Our world is full of divisions everywhere—divisions between nations, divisions between power blocs, divisions between colour and party, divisions between employer and employed, divisions between individuals that can result in hatred and jealousy. Again, science is discovering what a wonderful universe this is, and is enabling its resources to be developed for human use. But scientific discovery and invention can accentuate human divisions. One nation may try to beat another in the exploitation of what scientific research uncovers, or, through fear of each other, different nations may use the discoveries of science for building more and more effective weapons of destruction. The individual human personality is itself the scene of 'division'. It can rise to the heights of love, self-sacrifice, generosity, and noble thoughts and action. But it can also sink to the depths of ugliness, hatred, pride and revenge. In the individual life there can be the battleground of a pull between the noblest and the lowest.

The Roman poet Ovid (first century B.C.) said, 'I see the better course and I approve it; but the worse is the one I follow.' Paul speaks in the same vein in Rom. 7: 19, 'The good which I want to do, I fail to do; but what I do is the wrong which is against my will.' Modern psychology has also shown how complicated the individual personality can be; there can be a serious conflict between what it calls the organized self and the disorganized self. The latter consists of the impulses that arise from repressed complexes and suppressed instincts. There is need of an 'ideal' to act as a magnet to draw the personality together.

In the midst of this picture of these divisions at different levels, questions such as the following arise: Is there a 'something' which can break down these cleavages, and provide a way of surmounting these divisions? Is there a 'rallying point' where the universe and human life can find a common denominator and a unity? Is there a common purpose or aim that ought to underlie all human action and endeavour? People have all sorts of allegiances and loyalties; but is there one basic loyalty underlying all others? Is there a starting-point from which we are to understand human life on this planet?

Ephesians confronts us with the challenge that such a 'rallying point' has been provided. God 'has made known to us his hidden purpose...namely that the universe, all in heaven and earth, might be brought into a unity in Christ' (1: 10). In the ministry of Jesus Christ the claim is staked that God and his love for his world are what ultimately matter (4: 6, 'one God and Father of all who is over all and through all and in all'). Therefore the depth of possibility for human life is plumbed only when people try to respond to that love at all levels and see its implications: (i) for all kinds of human relationships, (ii) for the right use of the resources of God's universe, and (iii) for resistance to all that is opposed to that love. Allegiance to Jesus Christ and to the view of the world which he represents means that there is a common meeting place, where human beings meet on neutral ground, not subject to prejudices of nation, colour and class. To believe that all men are brothers in the service of the One God is a challenge to human divisions. The magnet of the sacrificial and self-giving love of God seen in Jesus Christ can give the individual life a common aim, and draw the best out of it, providing that 'ideal' of which the psychologists talk. The Church at the world-wide level, and at the level of the local congregation, is to be a fellowship witnessing in all possible ways to this common 'rallying point'. In this sense Christians (as is the claim of Ephesians) have the light and are the light in which human rejection of God's love is to be exposed (5: 7-8, 'For though you were once all darkness, now as Christians you are light. Live like men who are at home in daylight').

(2) *Human Equality*

It is a common saying that all men are or should be equal This needs further definition. It cannot mean that all are equal in the sense that all have the same capacities and gifts;

it does not suggest that all have the same amount of material possessions, or that there are to be no such people as leaders. The saying is trying to make the point that all human personalities, whatever their colour, status, class or background are to be respected and valued and given the opportunity to develop. 'All men are equal' carries with it the result that all races have a right to a fair share of the world's resources and the opportunities for living a full human life. It is a denial of any theory of a 'master' or 'super' race, based on the idea that one race is 'destined' or 'entitled' to dominate another. For example, the West may have developed technically more rapidly than other peoples, but that does not mean that Western man has an intrinsic superiority and the right to dominate others. It means rather a responsibility and privilege to use his more advanced knowledge of the scientific world to improve the conditions of others and help forward their way of life.

But the question might be asked: on what is this theory of the 'equality of man' based? Ephesians contains the Christian answer. Paul was as aware as anyone of the religious and social distinctions between human beings (e.g. Col. 3: 11, 'Greek and Jew, circumcised and uncircumcised, barbarian, Scythian, freeman, slave'). As a Jew he knew the great distinction between Jew and non-Jew (see Eph. 2: 11, 'Remember then your former condition: you, Gentiles as you are outwardly, you, "the uncircumcised" so called by those who are called "the circumcised"').

But this distinctiveness of the Jewish religion did not mean that the Jews were a 'master' race; the Jewish privilege was only part of God's plan of preparation for the coming of Jesus Christ. For Paul there is one thing that creates the equality of man, and this is the work of Jesus Christ who summons men to a loving relationship with God and therefore with each other (Eph. 2: 15, 'so as to create a single new humanity in himself, thereby making peace'). It is this common 'access' to God that gives human beings their value.

In other words, human equality is something God-made and not man-made.

(3) The Problem of evil

One of the strengths of the Christian approach to life has been the realistic attitude shown towards evil in its various forms of ugliness, suffering, ignorance, and moral evil. In Christian thought, from the earliest days, evil has never been regarded as an illusion, but has been faced squarely, despite some of the problems that it raises for belief in a God of love. By his reference to 'superhuman forces of evil in the heavens' (6: 12), Paul underlines the fact that evil is a very real thing in this world. Some kinds of evil can be traced to the free choice which human beings have, within certain limits, for ordering their lives and developing the world around them. People can spoil their relationships with others, and can use the world's resources selfishly. Paul speaks of the attitude that can lead to this state of affairs when he describes men as following 'the evil ways of this present age' (2: 2) and as obeying 'the promptings' of their own 'instincts and notions' (2: 3). Other forms of evil, such as painful suffering and illness, sometimes of the young and innocent, are less easy to understand, and may pose the question: 'How can a universe where this sort of thing happens have a God of love as its heart and centre?'

While there is much about this problem that we cannot understand, the Letter to the Ephesians does make several useful contributions to the subject:

(a) The letter stresses Jesus Christ as the point where the world finds its unity, and so presents the challenge: perhaps the question should not be 'How in the face of the evidence of human suffering and other heartless features of human life can I believe in a God of love?' *but* 'How after the vision of God in Jesus Christ can one help believing in the love of God despite the contrary evidence?' Though it is true that there is much in this problem that we do not understand, people have held to their belief in God's love despite their suffering. Such faith has sustained them and helped them to 'redeem' their sufferings, in the sense that they have refused to become bitter about them.

(b) The God of whom Paul speaks in Ephesians is not one remote from everyday life. In Jesus Christ he has shared human life and entered into its distresses and sorrows. Paul brings this out by his references to the 'shedding of the blood' of Jesus Christ (1: 7, 'For in Christ our release is secured and our sins are forgiven through the shedding of his blood').

(c) Evil in all its forms is to be attacked with all possible methods that are in accordance with the mind and purpose of God as revealed in Jesus Christ (6: 11, 'Put on all the armour which God provides'). It is to be seen as something marring God's creation. This applies, for example, to disease or illness, which must not directly or by implication be attributed to God. Jesus' acts of healing, described in the Gospels, contradict the idea that illness is 'God's visitation'. Disease is to be fought with weapons, which include prayer but also the work of doctors, hospitals and medical research. In Eph 6: 17, the Christian 'sword' consists of 'the words that come from God' and among these words is the command of Gen. 1: 28 ('...fill the earth and subdue it...' R.S.V.). God's invitation to scientific research and the development of the world's resources.

Ephesians therefore faces us with the fact that evil is something very real. It is something that conflicts with the love of God, who will, despite all, work out his purposes for his world. We co-operate with those purposes by taking a positive approach towards evil, and uprooting it with all the weapons that he has given us. 'Use the present opportunity to the full, for these are evil days' (5: 16).

✻   ✻   ✻   ✻   ✻   ✻   ✻   ✻   ✻   ✻   ✻   ✻   ✻

THE LETTER OF PAUL TO

THE COLOSSIANS

✷ ✷ ✷ ✷ ✷ ✷ ✷ ✷ ✷ ✷ ✷ ✷ ✷ ✷

THE EARLY HISTORY OF THE LETTER

The evidence of the Revelation of John might suggest that the letter to the Colossians was known and valued by A.D. 96 (see above, p. 2). In any case it had a place in collections of Paul's letters which were known and used in the period A.D. 100–150. For example, Bishop Ignatius of Antioch, who was martyred at Rome in the time of the Emperor Trajan (A.D. 98–117) wrote a letter to the church at Ephesus and told them to be 'steadfast in the faith' (10: 2). This sounds like an echo of Col. 1: 23, which is translated in the N.E.B.: 'Only you must continue in your faith, firm on your foundations, never to be dislodged.' Similarly in a letter to the church at Tralles, a place in Asia Minor (see map, p. ix), he uses the phrase 'visible and invisible' (5: 2) in a context where angels and powers are also mentioned: 'though I am in bonds and can understand heavenly things, and the places of the angels and the gatherings of powers, and things visible and invisible'. This is probably reminiscent of Col. 1: 16, 'In him everything in heaven and on earth was created, not only things visible but also the invisible orders of thrones, sovereignties, authorities and powers.' So when Ignatius (in his letter to the Ephesians, 12: 2) speaks of 'every letter' of Paul he no doubt includes among them the letter to the Colossians. Moreover, to reinforce his protest about the Church's use of the Old Testament (A.D. 140–160), Marcion of Sinope was able to use an already existing collection of Paul's letters, which included Colossians, and edit them to suit his views (see above, p. 3). It is clear that well before A.D. 150, Colossians had a recognized place among the letters of Paul and was regarded as an authoritative writing for the guidance of the Church.

WAS PAUL THE AUTHOR?

The senses in which Paul may be regarded as the author of a letter have already been discussed (above, p. 5). The opening sentence of Colossians claims that the letter was written, dictated or commissioned by Paul (1:1, 'From Paul, apostle of Christ Jesus...'). This fact was never in any doubt in the early Church, and it was the authority of Paul behind the letter that gave it its importance.

More recently, difficulties have been raised about attributing the letter to Paul. It has therefore sometimes been regarded as 'pseudonymous', i.e. written in the name of Paul after his death by a devoted disciple. (For this kind of writing see above, p. 4.)

As with Ephesians, we have to ask the question: Can Paul be regarded as the author of Colossians, or is there something about the letter that demands that it must have been written after his death?

WHAT ARE THE PROBLEMS?

(1) *Language*

The language of Colossians has much in common with that of Paul's other letters, though some of Paul's familiar words and phrases are missing. For example his well-known expression 'to be justified by faith' is not found in Colossians. But this is not surprising, because this expression is common only where Paul is fighting the claim that we can by our own efforts put ourselves right with God (e.g. in Galatians). The situation being faced at Colossae is of a very different kind. It is worth recalling that the phrase is not used in 1 Thessalonians. On the other hand a large number of new words and phrases occur, which are not found in such earlier letters as Romans, 1 and 2 Corinthians, Galatians and 1 Thessalonians.

Some examples are as follows:

'heritage'	(1: 12)
'complete being of God'	(1: 19)
'making peace'	(1: 20)
'complete the full tale'	(1: 24)
'persuasive words'	(2: 4)
'captured'	(2: 8)
'embodied'	(2: 9)
'bond'	(2: 14)
'new moon'	(2: 16)
'angel-worship'	(2: 18)
'severity to the body'	(2: 23)
'be arbiter'	(3: 15)
'to curry favour with men'	(3: 22)
'never insipid'	(4: 6)

But, as we saw in our discussion of the language of Ephesians (above, p. 7), the occurrence of new words and phrases can be a very insecure guide in deciding whether a work is written by a particular author. For example, it is difficult to judge from the amount of Paul's writing that has survived how rich and wide his vocabulary might be. The range of a writer's vocabulary can also be extended by his own widening experience, and new words may be brought into use in new situations. For example, terms may be taken up from the people against whom one is arguing. Such phrases as 'the complete being of Godhead' (2: 9), 'angel-worship' (2: 18), 'new moon' (2: 16) and 'severity to the body' (2: 23) are probably all called out by the situation being faced. Terms of this kind were probably being used in the propaganda of those who were trying to persuade the Colossian Christians to compromise and combine their faith in Jesus with faith in other powers (see below, p. 121). Some of the new terms may also be due to the fact that in the circumstances in which

Colossians was written a fair amount of scope was given to Paul's secretary or representative. Perhaps this is why Paul draws attention to his imprisonment at the end of the letter (4: 18, 'Remember that I am in prison'). It must not be ruled out that Timothy, Paul's trusted 'colleague' for some years past, made a contribution towards the composition of the letter. He is associated with Paul in the opening greeting of the letter (1: 1, 'From Paul...and our colleague Timothy').

(2) *Style*

The general impression left by the Greek style of Colossians is that it is very ragged. The construction of the sentences is very loose and does not always take account of strict grammar. A bewildering number of participles are used. In the English of the N.E.B. this raggedness cannot be so much appreciated, as it is smoothed out in the interest of clarity. We may use as an example 1: 9–12: 'For this reason, ever since the day we heard of it, we have not ceased to pray for you. We ask God that you may receive from him all wisdom and spiritual understanding for full insight into his will, so that your manner of life may be worthy of the Lord and entirely pleasing to him. We pray that you may bear fruit in active goodness of every kind, and grow in the knowledge of God. May he strengthen you, in his glorious might, with ample power to meet whatever comes with fortitude, patience, and joy; and to give thanks to the Father who has made you fit to share the heritage of God's people in the realm of light.' The involved nature of this section can be seen to some extent in the English, but in the Greek it is part of one long sentence, which has been split up into four sentences in the translation. Again, in the Greek, 'ask', 'bear fruit', 'grow', 'strengthen' and 'give thanks' are all participles loosely strung together. Something of the involved nature of the style can also be seen in 1: 24, which in the Greek is the beginning of one long sentence: 'It is now my happiness to suffer for you. This is my way of helping to complete, in my poor human flesh, the full tale of Christ's afflictions still to be endured, for the sake of his body which is the church.'

The style of Colossians is therefore contrasted with the more rapid flow and clearer sequence of the language of the earlier letters. It would be wrong, however, to say that the style of Paul's earlier letters is always tidy and even. For example, 2 Cor. 9: 12–14 is a single sentence in the Greek and its construction is of the loosest: 'for as a piece of willing service this is not only a contribution towards the needs of God's people; more than that, it overflows in a flood of thanksgiving to God. For through the proof which this affords, many will give honour to God when they see how humbly you obey him and how faithfully you confess the gospel of Christ; and will thank him for your liberal contribution to their need and to the general good. And as they join in prayer on your behalf, their hearts will go out to you because of the richness of the grace which God has imparted to you.' The ragged style of Colossians could be due to the haste with which Paul dictated the letter, or the tension under which he laboured, as he tried to deal with the critical situation at Colossae from his own distant imprisonment at Rome. The composition may also owe something to the work of Timothy, as we saw previously in discussing the language of the letter. But it is not possible from the style alone to draw any conclusion that Colossians was written after the death of Paul.

(3) *Some supposed differences of theological thought and expression*

It is pointed out that the Christology of Colossians, i.e. the view of the person of Jesus and his significance, is more clearly defined and formulated than in Paul's earlier letters. Some other terms such as 'reconciliation' are used in a different way, and the relationship between Jesus and the Church is described in different terms. We now consider some of these subjects.

(a) *The Person of Jesus.* In 1: 15–17 the unique status of

Jesus is described: 'He is the image of the invisible God; his is the primacy over all created things. In him everything in heaven and on earth was created, not only things visible but also the invisible orders of thrones, sovereignties, authorities, and powers: the whole universe has been created through him and for him. And he exists before everything, and all things are held together in him.' Here Jesus is seen as the one through whom the whole created order came into being, the one who sustains all existence, and the one in whom the world is to find its meaning. The language is very much like that used by Jewish writers to describe the function of God's Word and Wisdom. The latter were ways of referring to a power or activity of God through which he made the world, keeps it in being, and reveals himself. For example, the Wisdom of Solomon in the Apocrypha, a Jewish work probably written in the first century A.D., describes God's Wisdom:

> 'For wisdom is more mobile than any motion;
> Yea, she pervadeth and penetrateth all things
>   by reason of her pureness.
> For she is a breath of the power of God,
> And a clear effluence of the glory of the Almighty.
> Therefore can nothing defiled find entrance into her.
> For she is an effulgence from everlasting light,
> And an unspotted mirror of the working of God,
> And an image of his goodness.
> And she, being one, hath power to do all things;
> And remaining in herself, reneweth all things;
> And from generation to generation passing into
>   holy souls
> She maketh men friends of God and prophets.'

(7: 24–7)

In Wisd. of Sol. 9: 1–2 the ideas of God's Word and Wisdom are brought together:

> 'O God of the Fathers, and Lord who keepest
>   thy mercy,

108

> Who madest all things by thy word;
> And by thy wisdom thou formedst man.'

In the thought of Philo, the Jewish thinker and theologian of Alexandria (born 20 B.C.), and a contemporary of Jesus and Paul, the Word of God is very important as the means by which God creates and remains in contact with his world. Philo calls it 'the image of God' (*De Confusione Linguarum*, 97. 147) and 'the captain and steersman of the universe' (*De Cherubim*, 36). It is a sign of the deep impression made on his early disciples by Jesus that they applied to him the status and activity of God's Word or Wisdom. In this way they saw that Jesus was the one who could be God's agent in *reclaiming* the world precisely because he was the one through whom the world was created and sustained.

In Col. 1: 15–17 Jesus is clearly thought of as God's Word or Wisdom, though these words are not actually used. The language used here of Jesus is sometimes considered to be more developed than in the earlier letters of Paul. But Paul had already equated Jesus with God's Word or Wisdom. In 1 Cor. 1: 30 he says that 'God has made him (Jesus) our wisdom', and in 1 Cor. 8: 6 speaks of 'Jesus Christ through whom all things came to be', language that could be used of God's Word. The same idea is found in 2 Cor. 4: 4, where Jesus is described as 'the very image of God'. These references show that Paul in his earlier letters understands Jesus to be God's Word or Wisdom, though in the situations in which he wrote he had no need to elaborate the idea further. But in Colossians much more emphasis is placed on this status of Jesus, in order to underline that he is the one and only way to God. This, as we shall see, is part of Paul's answer to the propaganda of those who were saying that faith in Jesus should be combined with faith in other powers of the universe. Further, because of this status of Jesus, Paul can say that 'in Christ... the complete being of the Godhead dwells', i.e. in him one is confronted with the divine power behind the universe, the power that matters. The view of the person of Jesus in Colossians is only an elaboration of the importance attached to him in Paul's earlier letters.

(b) *The use of the term 'reconciliation'.* In the earlier letters Paul speaks of *men* being reconciled to God through the mission of Jesus (e.g. Rom. 5: 11, 'we also exult in God through our Lord Jesus, through whom we have now been granted reconciliation'). In Colossians Paul uses the word like this in 1: 22, 'But now by Christ's death...God has reconciled you to himself.' But he also employs 'reconcile' in a wider way to describe the fact that God restores not only human beings but also superhuman forces to himself (1: 20, 'Through him God chose to reconcile the whole universe to himself...to reconcile all things, whether on earth or in heaven...'). Similarly the cross is concerned with the defeat of superhuman powers of evil (2: 15, 'On that cross he discarded the cosmic powers and authorities like a garment').

It has sometimes been thought that this approach to Jesus' work is not in accordance with the teaching contained in Paul's earlier letters. But 'reconcile' is used in the wider sense at 2 Cor. 5: 19, 'What I mean is, that God was in Christ reconciling the world to himself.' Here the term 'world', as used by Paul, includes not only human beings but also forces of evil that have gained a grip on God's universe. Similarly Jesus' defeat of these powers is implied in 1 Cor. 2: 8, 'The powers that rule the world have never known it; if they had, they would not have crucified the Lord of glory,' where the 'powers' mentioned probably refer to superhuman evil forces. The same point is made explicitly in Rom. 8: 38, 'For I am convinced that there is nothing in death or life, in the realm of spirits or superhuman powers...that can separate us from the love of God in Christ Jesus our Lord.' The thought of Colossians in this respect is in line with that of Paul's earlier letters.

(c) *The use of 'the head' and 'the body' to describe the relationship between Jesus and the Church.* It is pointed out that this

terminology is not used in Paul's earlier letters. His usual way
is to think of Jesus as 'the body' or organism, while Christians
form the parts of the organism (e.g. 1 Cor. 12: 12, 'For
Christ is like a single body with its many limbs and organs,
which, many as they are, together make up one body').
But in certain passages of Colossians the church is described
as 'the body' and Jesus as its 'head'. In 1: 18 Jesus is described
as 'the head of the body, the church', while in 1: 24 we have
the phrase 'for the sake of his body which is the church.' It is
necessary to remember that a writer is not tied to his earlier
terminology, and when occasion arises he may wish to alter it.
In Colossians Paul is stressing that the *only* loyalty that matters
is that to Jesus, who *alone* can bring men into a living relationship with God. Paul had used the 'body' language earlier to
stress that all Christians have a part to play in the life and work
of the Church. Now, however, he wishes to underline the
lordship of Jesus, and so he varies the method of expression.
The word 'body' was in use to describe a community or
entity to which men belonged. The Stoics used the term to
describe 'the world'. Seneca, the Roman politician and philosopher (see above, p. 83) could say, 'We are members of a
great body' (*Letters* 95: 52). The word 'head' was sometimes
associated with the term 'body' to denote its controlling force. It
would therefore not be unnatural for Paul to make use of these
expressions to stress Jesus' unique status in relation to the Church.

To sum up: There is nothing in the language, style and
theological thought of Colossians that prevents us from holding the view that the letter belongs to Paul's lifetime. If not
dictated by him word for word, it can at least be regarded as
having been commissioned by him.

COLOSSAE

In the first century A.D. Colossae was a town in the Roman
Province of Asia, which was controlled by a Roman Governor,
called a proconsul, with headquarters in Ephesus. Colossae

lay on the main road from Ephesus to the East. This road went along the course of the Meander River as far as its junction with the tributary river Lycus (see map, p. ix). It then followed the latter river, passing after a few miles through Laodicea (Col. 4: 15), with Hierapolis (Col. 4: 13) ten miles to the north, and through Colossae, twelve miles further east. Colossae was therefore in the valley of the Lycus River, the latter running through the town in a deep ravine.

Colossae (or Colassae, as it was also popularly called) may have gained its name from a lake called Koloe. Herodotus, the Greek historian of the fifth century B.C., tells us that it was a great city of Phrygia, one of the places where King Xerxes halted his army before the invasion of Greece (480 B.C.). A little later Xenophon, the historian and writer of the fourth century B.C., records that it was 'a populous city, prosperous and great'. By the first century A.D. it had declined in size and importance. For example, Strabo, the writer on history and geography at the end of the first century B.C. and the beginning of the first century A.D., says that at this time Colossae was a small town in the district of which Laodicea was the centre. Shortly after Paul wrote Colossians the town was ruined by an earthquake, and its site was not identified until the nineteenth century. Excavation has revealed very little, except part of a theatre and an acropolis. The district bred large flocks of sheep and the minerals there provided materials for the dyers. Colossae probably had a guild of dyers like Hierapolis and Laodicea, for it gave its name to a rich purple dye known as 'colossinus'.

THE FOUNDATION OF THE CHURCH AT COLOSSAE

Paul was deeply interested in the Christians of Colossae. The Church there, however, had not arisen as the result of Paul's own work, but was to be traced to the efforts of Epaphras, one of his trusted fellow-workers (1: 7). It was from the latter that Paul had learnt of the deep loyalty of the Colossian

Christians (1: 8). That Paul had never visited Colossae or Laodicea is also shown by 2: 1 ('for you...and all who have never set eyes on me'). From Acts 16: 6, it appears that Paul, during the journey that he undertook after the Council of Jerusalem, intended to travel through the Lycus valley into Asia, but had been prevented by divine guidance of some kind. On his later journey from Palestine to Ephesus (Acts 18: 23; 19: 1) Paul probably passed to the north of the Lycus valley.

In the Acts of the Apostles Luke does not record the founding of the churches in this area. His purpose is not to give a complete history of the early years of the Church, but to describe the broad sweep of Christian missionary activity by which Christianity spread from Jerusalem to Rome. But he does pinpoint the importance of Paul's ministry and activity in Ephesus (Acts 19), which appear to have lasted about three years. We note, in Acts 19: 26, the slightly exaggerated declaration of Demetrius, the silversmith, which may, nevertheless, have been near the mark: 'And you see and hear how this fellow Paul with his propaganda has perverted crowds of people, not only at Ephesus but also in practically the whole province of Asia'. In other words, Paul was using Ephesus as a strategic centre for spreading the Gospel all through the province of Asia. In this work he was using such assistants as Timothy (below, p. 128), Tychicus, (below, p. 161), Epaphras (below, p. 130) and others. It can therefore easily be seen how in this period Christianity gained a hold in the Lycus valley, which had close connections with Ephesus. Epaphras himself was a native of Colossae (4: 12) and may have met Paul and heard the Gospel while on business in Ephesus.

WHERE WAS COLOSSIANS WRITTEN?

The letter itself does not tell us the place from which Paul is writing. All we know of his situation is that he is in prison (4: 18, 'Remember that I am in prison'). He also refers to his imprisonment in 1: 24, 'It is now my happiness to suffer for you.' There is a strong tradition that Colossians was written from Rome during the imprisonment of Paul described in Acts 28: 16, 'When we entered Rome Paul was allowed to lodge by himself with a soldier in charge of him.' This imprisonment lasted at least two years (Acts 28: 30, 'He stayed there two full years at his own expense'). An introduction to Colossians about A.D. 180 suggests Ephesus as the place of writing, but this is exceptional.

In more recent times several arguments have been brought forward against the firm tradition that Colossians was written at Rome, and may be briefly mentioned here.

(i) Colossians and the letter to Philemon are closely related to each other, and must have been written in the same period. For example, the letter to Philemon is about the runaway slave, Onesimus, who has joined Paul, and is being sent back by the latter to his master, Philemon. This links up with Col. 4: 9, 'With him (Tychicus) comes Onesimus, our trustworthy and dear brother.' Again, the names of those who are with Paul and send greetings at the conclusion of the letter to Philemon are Epaphras, Mark, Aristarchus, Demas and Luke (verses 23–24). They occur also in the greetings at the end of Colossians (4: 10–14). Another connection between the letters is the mention of Archippus (Philem. 2), for whom Paul also has a 'special word' in Col. 4: 17. These connections make it clear that the two letters date to about the same time. But it is sometimes thought more reasonable to suppose that Onesimus made his escape to somewhere like Caesarea or Ephesus (places much nearer to Colossae, see map, p. ix). It is easier to understand that Onesimus joined Paul at one of these places than to imagine that he made the long journey to Rome. If such a view is plausible, then we should have to say that both letters were sent during an imprisonment at Caesarea or Ephesus. There is evidence for Paul's imprisonment at Caesarea (Acts 23: 33–35, 'The cavalry entered Caesarea, delivered the letter to the Governor, and handed Paul over to him...He then ordered him to be held in custody at his headquarters in Herod's palace'). The evidence that Paul was put in prison at Ephesus is not strong. We know that Paul suffered a number of imprisonments, probably more than are described in the New Testament (2 Cor. 11: 23). These *may* have included one at Ephesus. Paul went through a very perilous time there, which he describes, for example, in the vivid language of having 'fought wild beasts' (1 Cor. 15: 32). But nowhere in references to this dangerous period of his ministry (e.g. 2 Cor. 1: 8–10) does he mention an actual imprisonment, nor is the later evidence at all conclusive.

It may, however, seem plausible to think that Colossians and Philemon were written from Caesarea. But on the other hand it is easy to underestimate the facilities for travel in the ancient world. Philem. 18 implies that Onesimus had robbed his master of money, and he may well have used some of this to book himself a passage for Rome! Here he may have thought that he could remain hidden much more satisfactorily than in Asia Minor.

(ii) In Philem. 22 Paul expresses the hope of paying an early visit to Colossae: 'have a room ready for me, for I hope that, in answer to your prayers, God will grant me to you.' This is considered to be more natural if he was in prison in Asia Minor than if he was in Rome, where his attention was concentrated on a visit to Spain in the event of his liberation. It is true that Paul, writing his letter to the Romans, looks forward to his coming visit to Spain and says: 'So when I have finished this business and delivered the proceeds under my own seal, I shall set out for Spain by way of your city' (15: 28). But when Paul expressed his intention, he did not know that he would go to Rome as a prisoner, and in Rome he may well have changed his plans about what he would do when he was freed. He may have thought that a visit to Asia Minor should have priority over a visit to Spain. The question of distance from Colossae would not have daunted him, any more than the distance from Spain.

(iii) Appeal has also been made to the difference in atmosphere between the letter to the Colossians and that to the Philippians. For example, it is said that in Philippians Paul writes hopefully and cheerfully about his imprisonment, while in Colossians he finds his confinement more trying. Therefore two different occasions of imprisonment are involved. Philippians may be left in its Roman setting, but Colossians should be assigned to an earlier imprisonment at, e.g. Caesarea. Too much could be made of the difference of atmosphere between the two letters, as this could be accounted for by the different situations being faced. Further, Paul says so little in Colossians about his imprisonment that it is difficult to know whether or not he found it more trying.

None of the arguments above is conclusive against the firm tradition that Colossians was written from Rome. This still remains the best possibility, and here it is accepted that both Colossians and Philemon belong to the imprisonment in Rome, the beginning of which is described in Acts 28: 16. In the same period (as already suggested above, p. 19) the manifesto, the Letter to the Ephesians, was issued for use in the Christian churches of Asia Minor. Travel facilities were so good in the Roman Empire that it is not hard to imagine Tychicus (Col. 4: 7) travelling between Asia Minor and Rome to keep Paul informed of what was happening. It was probably Tychicus who conveyed our present letter to Colossae.

WHEN WAS COLOSSIANS WRITTEN?

If the letter was written from Rome, its date will depend on the time of Paul's imprisonment at Rome which is described at the end of Acts, and is most probably to be placed in the period A.D. 59 onwards. The length of this imprisonment must remain uncertain.

Of relevance here is the date of the earthquake which is recorded by the Roman historian Tacitus, writing in the time of the Emperor Trajan (A.D. 98–117), and which devastated

Laodicea in A.D. 60. Eusebius (the church historian of the fourth century A.D. and Bishop of Caesarea) speaks of a similar disaster which also hit Colossae and Hierapolis. He assigns the event to the period immediately after the burning of Rome in A.D. 64. The difference in date may be due to error on the part of one of the historians, or there may have been two such disasters. If Colossians was written after a serious earthquake disaster in that area, there would be almost certainly some reference to it. It is also unlikely that immediately after such an occurrence religious controversy would have loomed so large, unless it arose from those who said that neglect of the planetary powers (see below, p. 119) was what had brought on the earthquake. Evidence for this is, however, lacking. If, therefore, Tacitus' dating is right, a date for Colossians before A.D. 60 is likely. If there was a single earthquake in A.D. 64 or shortly afterwards, a later date would be possible.

COLOSSAE: THE RELIGIOUS BACKGROUND

(1) *The 'all religions have something to offer' attitude*

This viewpoint was known as 'religious syncretism'. It had been encouraged by the spirit of religious toleration that marked Alexander the Great and his successors. Alexander succeeded his father Philip as King of Macedon in 336 B.C. Philip had created a union of the Greek states, and Alexander extended his power by conquest of the Persian Empire and Egypt. On his death there was no one man strong enough to hold the empire together, and after a period of struggle three great powers had emerged by the year 276 B.C.: the house of Ptolemy in Egypt, the house of Seleucus in Asia, and the house of Antigonus in Macedonia. Alexander's conquests brought the East and West into a closer relation, which in turn had an effect on religion. The different gods and goddesses were thought to be the same under different names. The goddess Isis was believed to be worshipped throughout the world under different names with different rites. She was revered by the Athenians as Athene, in Crete she was worshipped as Artemis, in Cyprus as Aphrodite.

In the period 300 B.C.–A.D. 200, the different religious cults borrowed from each other and adopted each other's features, ideas and practices. Of particular interest here is the cult of the god Sabazios, because its centre was in Phrygia, the area round Colossae. Sabazios was given the attributes and characteristics of such gods as Zeus, Dionysos, Mithra and fertility and underworld deities. Some Jews of Phrygia combined the worship of Sabazios with that of their national God, Yahweh; the latter's title, Sabaoth, no doubt helped the equation. This was a very unusual practice for Jews. The same applies to the fact that Jewesses are found as priestesses in the service of certain Phrygian goddesses. This illustrates how strongly people in the area round Colossae felt that all religions had something to offer and should be combined together. (See further The 'Cult of Sabazios', by W. O. E. Oesterley, in *The Labyrinth*, ed. S. H. Hooke, S.P.C.K., pp. 115–58.)

(2) *The Mystery religions*

The older forms of religion, such as the worship of the Olympian gods, had by this time become just a respectable convention, to which lip-service was paid. People of the first century A.D. were obsessed with fear of the world around them. They felt surrounded by hostile forces and demons, bringing with them misfortunes and diseases. Human beings were believed to be persecuted for a sin committed by some ancestor of the human race. A sense of futility and failure was rife. The planets and signs of the Zodiac were thought to be divine beings which had power for good or evil over human destiny. The body was held to be evil, a prison from which men needed to be freed. In face of this human helplessness, the so-called 'Mystery cults' offered hope and encouragement.

All these cults, as the name 'mystery' implies, practised secret rites into which people were initiated. In this way they were freed from the dangers, darkness and ignorance of a world dominated by evil, and so passed into a state of enlightenment, privilege and hope of immortality. These rites, based on old myths and legends about divine beings, sometimes included a sacred meal or sacred marriage. The aim was to be united with the god or goddess in death and resurrection. This brought escape from one's present evil environment. The members of the cult met for the celebration of the 'Mysteries'. This might include the whitening and chalking of faces, sprinkling with the contents of a cup, and the singing of songs and clashing of timbrels. In the Sabazios cult a meal played an important part; this was thought to be an anticipation of a heavenly banquet which awaited the initiates after death. Some of the Mystery cults demanded a long course of training, very strict discipline and severe tests. These cults were attractive because people believed in the magical power of secret rites. They offered excitement in a rather drab existence, and held out the warmth and 'togetherness' that membership of a fellowship brings.

THE DANGER FACING THE COLOSSIAN CHURCH

The situation that led Paul to write Colossians is not known to us in detail. He is writing to those who are directly involved and know the circumstances for themselves. But evidence, direct and indirect, helps us to draw certain conclusions.

(1) *The direct evidence*

Some kind of subversive propaganda was going on in the Colossian Church (see 2: 4, 'being talked into error by specious arguments'). This is said to derive from 'hollow and delusive speculations, based on traditions of man-made teaching and centred on the elemental spirits of the world' (2: 8). The 'speculations' may be the legends on which some of the Mystery cults were based. We know that the latter were concerned with giving protection against the 'elemental spirits' or planetary powers. Various kinds of self-denial and abstention from certain foods and drinks were being urged upon the Christian congregation (2: 16, 20–1, 'Allow no one therefore to take you to task about what you eat or drink... Why let people dictate to you: "Do not handle this, do not taste that, do not touch the other..."?'). These remind one of the Mysteries. Some of the religious practices mentioned in 2: 16 also sound very Jewish ('...the observance of festival, new moon, or sabbath'). We have to bear in mind that disloyal Jews were to be found among the followers of the Sabazios cult. Probably the Colossian Church is being challenged by propaganda from a Mystery religion flavoured with Jewish ideas.

Those who were bringing pressure to bear on the Colossian Church also practised, it seems, some kind of 'angel-worship' (2: 18, 'You are not to be disqualified by the decision of people who go in for self-mortification and angel-worship'). It was not the Jewish custom to worship angels, though they regarded them as important intermediaries between God and man. 'Angels' here may be another way of describing the planetary powers. In the 'Sabazios' cult however, the god, Mercury, was described as the 'Good Angel', who conducted the dead to the feast of the blessed. It may be that angels had some other part in the belief and practice of this and other cults. The mention of 'vision' in the same passage could be a reference to the secret rites of the Mysteries and the experiences offered through them.

(2) *The indirect evidence*

It is striking that all through Colossians Paul stresses the uniqueness and all-sufficiency of Jesus Christ to give security. He can have no rivals. In 1: 15–20 Jesus, as God's word (see above, p. 108), is viewed as the key figure: (*a*) in the creation of the world and its maintenance; and (*b*) in the reclaiming of it for God. His supreme position in relation to all other forces and powers claiming to influence human destiny is stressed. In 2: 9–10, similarly, the supremacy of Jesus over all other 'power rivals', such as the planetary powers, is underlined

('For it is in Christ that the complete being of the Godhead dwells embodied, and in him you have been brought to completion. Every power and authority in the universe is subject to him as Head'). The Colossians are reminded that they owe their newly found hope and security solely to their union with Jesus Christ. The description of Jesus as the 'head' of the church (1: 18; 2: 19) emphasizes the *sole* allegiance that Christians owe to him. The same applies when he is viewed as the 'root' and 'foundation' (2: 7) and the one in whom '*all* God's treasures of wisdom' are available. All through the letter Paul asserts that only Jesus Christ can put people in touch with the God who matters and can bring reassurance to human fears.

Both the direct and indirect evidence suggests that the Colossian Church was being subjected to a propaganda line which said: 'All religions have their contribution to make, and so you can combine belief in Jesus Christ with the beliefs and practices of other cults. If you want the maximum insurance cover against the forces that control and endanger our existence, it is best to have a "comprehensive policy" including what other Mystery religions can offer.' This appeal probably came from the followers of neighbouring Mystery religions to which some of the Colossian Christians had (probably) belonged. The whole atmosphere of the time was against religious exclusiveness, and some of the Colossian Church may well have seen here an opportunity to commend Jesus Christ and his Gospel by gaining an entry for him into the other Mystery cults. This propaganda might also play on the fears of some of the Colossian Christians, who, though attracted by Jesus and his message, yet in their innermost hearts feared the consequences of deserting the religious practices in which they had been brought up.

THE COUNTER-ATTACK OF PAUL

(1) *The solid basis of Christianity*

The motives of the Mystery cults were often good. They were trying to bring reassurance and security to human beings. But the basis of these cults was only 'speculations' (2: 8), often the result of seeing deeper meanings in old legends and stories about gods and heroes. On the other hand, the Christian religion is solidly based on a *historical* person, Jesus Christ, who lived a human life and died a human death. It is here that men are confronted with 'the complete being' of God (1: 19, 'For in him the complete being of God...came to dwell'). God's hand of friendship is held out in a 'body of flesh and blood' (1: 22), and in the shedding of a historical person's blood upon the cross' (1: 20), the scene of Jesus' victory (2: 15). The use of 'Jesus' (the human name) in 2: 6 is also perhaps significant; it is the one who has lived as a historical character whom the Colossians believe in as Lord. In like manner Paul takes for granted as an established fact the resurrection of Jesus (2: 12–13; 3: 1, 'Were you not raised to life with Christ?'). Although he does not discuss this event in detail, he knows that the resurrection of Jesus is something that has been experienced and witnessed by *historical* people such as Peter and the other disciples, as well as himself.

(2) *Jesus, the only true route to God*

For the Mystery religions the world was a kind of closed system or prison, walled in by evil forces, which had to be broken through by various kinds of 'escape mechanism'. Physical death itself stood for the frustration and ineffectiveness of human life. Paul accepts as his starting-point this picture of a world ringed with forces that wish to exclude man from the true God in whom security is to be found. The best way of deliverance from this predicament is to be found in Jesus, who, unlike the mythical gods and goddesses, has lived with other human beings in this situation and has provided the answer.

How has this rescue 'from the domain of darkness' (1: 13) been achieved?

(*a*) The whole ministry of Jesus is shot through with the love and forgivingness of God (1: 20). In him the love of God breaks into this closed system.

(*b*) Jesus' life was untainted by the evil environment in which he lived. He was obedient to God even when such obedience led him to death by crucifixion, and his faith in God held firm right to the end (Luke 23: 46, 'Then Jesus gave a loud cry and said, "Father, into thy hands I commit my spirit"'). The 'cross' is therefore the victory described in 2: 15 ('On that cross he discarded the cosmic powers and authorities like a garment; he made a public spectacle of them and led them as captives in his triumphal procession'). Jesus' life and death are 'protests' against men's fears and anxieties and their helpless feeling of being in the grip of invisible forces.

(*c*) What has really achieved the 'break-through', however, is the fact that Jesus is 'the first to return from the dead' (1: 18). The execution of Jesus could suggest that, however wonderful he was, he had nevertheless become one more 'spent force'. But he appeared 'alive from the dead' to his disciples. This was God's way of showing that his career was not finished, but that he was still an effective force in the world. The 'closed system' had failed to hold or contain him. Jesus had made a 'come-back' and by his victory had broken the merciless grip of the forces (including death) that held men's minds in enslavement.

(3) *The status of Jesus*

The rescue operation carried out by Jesus is so much more reliable because it is made by one who is the true God's Word or Wisdom (see above, p. 109), through whom God made the world and keeps it in being (1: 15–17, 'He is the image of the invisible God; his is the primacy over all created things. In him everything in heaven and on earth was created, not only things visible but also the invisible orders of thrones, sovereignties, authorities and powers: the whole universe has been created through him and for him. And he exists before everything, and all things are held together in him'). He can therefore open up the way to the real power behind the world. In contrast, the forces that human beings fear, e.g. 'the invisible orders of thrones, sovereignties...' (1: 16), in whatever way they have gained their control over human minds, can only be part of the created world and owe their origin ultimately to Jesus.

(4) *Christian security*

This arises particularly from the knowledge that a reconciliation has been effected between God and his creation in Jesus. Human beings are therefore in touch with the only power in the universe that ultimately matters (1: 20–22, 'Through him God chose to reconcile the whole universe to himself, making peace through the shedding of his blood upon the cross...') and there is the opportunity of membership of God's people which is achieved through baptism (i.e. immersion in water). In this rite the Christian becomes identified with the 'break-through' of Jesus (2: 12, 'For in baptism you were buried with him, in baptism also you were raised to life with him through your faith in the active power of God who raised him from the dead'). In the first place, then, baptism stands for burial and death with Jesus (see also 2: 20), i.e. one associates oneself with 'the protest' of Jesus described above. Secondly, it means resurrection with Jesus (see also 3: 1), i.e. sharing with him in the life that is not restricted and hedged in by all kinds of fears. But baptism is not just something magical, it has to be accompanied by faith in God and his power to help us.

(5) *Christian 'release'*

Paul, with the Mystery religions, knows that people need release from all kinds of fears and slaveries. The most important 'release', however, is from a sense of guilt and the consciousness of not having lived up to what is known to be right (1: 21). It is this kind of freedom that is offered by the Christian Gospel (1: 13–14, 'He...brought us away into the kingdom of his dear Son, in whom our release is secured and our sins forgiven'). First, Jesus brings us the assurance of God's love and forgiveness with the offer of a new start (1: 21, 'Formerly you were yourselves estranged from God; you were his enemies in heart and mind, and your deeds were evil. But now by Christ's death in his body of flesh and blood God has reconciled you to himself'). Secondly, the victory of Jesus' obedience to God in the face of all obstacles brings encouragement in the midst of human failure (2: 14, 'he has cancelled the bond...It stood against us, but he has set it aside, nailing it to the cross').

(6) *Christian prospects*

All the Mystery cults held out a hope for the future, often in the form of immortality after death. Sometimes there is the picture of members being presented or conducted after death into the guest-chamber of the blessed to share their feast, after a favourable verdict has been pronounced on the dead person. In the Mithra cult the initiate is taken through various stages and brought finally into the presence of the supreme god. Similarly the prospect of Christians is to be 'presented' at God's court, as loyal citizens, worthy of his presence (1: 22, 'so that he may present you before himself as dedicated men, without blemish and innocent in his sight'). 'Hope' is a firm feature of the Christian Gospel (1: 23) and stems from union with Jesus (1: 27, 'Christ in you, the hope of a glory to come'). This 'glory' is a full life with Jesus, when God's will and purposes have been achieved (3: 4).

(7) *The Christian church—the Mystery religion with a world coverage*

Paul sees Christianity as a Mystery cult with a difference. It has a secret, but this is an open secret, which can be declared to the whole world (1: 25–27, 'I became its servant by virtue of the task assigned to me by God for your benefit...to announce the secret hidden for long ages and through many generations, but now disclosed to God's people, to whom it was his will to make it known—to make known how rich and glorious it is among the nations'). The world of Paul's day presented a series of divisions: the many and diverse mystery cults (though they did sometimes transcend tribe, city and class); the Jews (a race apart); the civilized nations as opposed to the uncivilized; the free as opposed to the slaves. Paul's claim is that Christianity is *the* one religion, where all these divisions can be broken down, and all types can meet (3: 11, 'There is no question here of Greek and Jew, circumcised and uncircumcised, barbarian, Scythian, freeman, slave; but Christ is all, and is in all'). Hence Paul's emphasis on the world-wide growth of the church (1: 6, 23).

(8) *Christianity and the present*

The Mysteries were very much concerned with securing one's future. They gave the appearance of encouraging escape from one's present life, though some of these religions did teach moral responsibility. Paul stresses that the Christian faith is not just concerned with securing the future, but has an important effect on life here and now. Initiation into the Christian cult involves a new beginning in the sense of developing the Christian character seen in Jesus of Nazareth (3: 9–10, 'now that you have discarded the old nature with its deeds and have put on the new nature') and in the discarding of conduct and standards that are unworthy of him and are often prevalent in contemporary society (3: 5–8). The qualities required of the Christian are given in 3: 12–13, 'Then put on the garments that suit God's chosen people, his own, his beloved: compassion, kindness, humility, gentleness, patience. Be forbearing with one another and forgiving, where any of you has cause for complaint: you must forgive as the Lord forgave you.' They can be summed up under the heading of 'love' (3: 14). Human relationships, too, have to be seen in a new light (3: 18 — 4: 1).

✳   ✳   ✳   ✳   ✳   ✳   ✳   ✳   ✳   ✳   ✳   ✳   ✳

The Centre of Christian Belief

OPENING GREETING

From Paul, apostle of Christ Jesus commissioned by **1** the will of God, and our colleague Timothy, to **2** God's people at Colossae, brothers in the faith, incorporate in Christ.

Grace to you and peace from God our Father.

✳ The opening follows the pattern of the other Pauline letters. (See on Eph. 1: 1–2.)

1. For the office and status of an apostle see above, p. 29. *will of God* stresses that Paul's position is not man-given, but a direct gift from God (Gal. 1: 1, 'Paul, an apostle, not by human appointment or human commission, but by commission from Jesus Christ and from God the Father'). As in other letters (e.g. 1 Thessalonians), Paul associates Timothy with himself in the sending of the letter. This may mean that Timothy also had a part in the composition of the letter (see above pp. 106–7). He is described as a *colleague* (Greek: 'brother') which usually means a fellow Christian; here it may also describe Paul's close association with Timothy in the Church's ministry.

Timothy had been a companion of Paul and co-worker with him since his second visit to Derbe and Lystra (Acts 16: 1–3). Timothy was the son of a Jewish Christian mother and a Greek father. He accompanied Paul on the journey that followed (Acts 17: 14). He played an important part in the preaching of the Gospel at Corinth (2 Cor. 1: 19), and was also sent on a mission to Thessalonica (1 Thess. 3: 2). Later, during the troubles in the Corinthian Church, Timothy was given the task of bringing the Corinthian Christians to a better frame of mind (1 Cor. 4: 17; 16: 10). He was also active in Macedonia (Acts 19: 22) and accompanied Paul on his journey to Jerusalem (Acts 20: 4). At some stage he was at Rome with Paul in the period when Colossians was written. The high regard in which he was held by Paul can be seen from Phil. 2: 20–23 ('There is no one else here who sees things as I do, and takes a genuine interest in your concerns; they are all bent on their own ends, not on the cause of Christ Jesus. But Timothy's record is known to you: you know that he has been at my side in the service of the Gospel like a son working under his father'). The two letters to Timothy are probably evidence that at a later stage he continued to be an important assistant of Paul.

2. *incorporate*, i.e. forming part of Jesus Christ, here regarded as a kind of organism to which people can belong and so share in the benefits that he has brought to the world.

Grace...Father is almost a prayer that the Colossians may share the full benefits of God's *grace*, i.e. his love and favour revealed in Jesus, and of his *peace*, i.e. his offer of friendship and reconciliation. Christians can address God as *our Father* because they are put in touch with him by Jesus and know his love. Jesus encouraged his disciples to address God as 'Father' (Matt. 6: 9; see also Gal 4: 6, 'To prove that you are sons, God has sent into our hearts the Spirit of his Son, crying "Abba! Father!"'). *Jesus* is the human name. *Christ* (literally 'the Anointed One') was originally a title, denoting Jesus as the expected King of the Jews. It then became part of his name.

'Lord' is a title of the risen and exalted Jesus. It describes his divinity and the allegiance that he expects from his followers, and depicts him as the one in whom God reclaims lordship over his world. For 'Lord Jesus Christ' see also above, p. 30. This close connection between God and Jesus led to rethinking about the nature of God, and to the formulation of the doctrine of the Trinity (see above, p. 64). ✻

THANKSGIVING

In all our prayers to God, the Father of our Lord Jesus 3 Christ, we thank him for you, because we have heard of 4 the faith you hold in Christ Jesus, and the love you bear towards all God's people. Both spring from the hope 5 stored up for you in heaven—that hope of which you learned when the message of the true Gospel first came 6 to you. In the same way it is coming to men the whole world over; everywhere it is growing and bearing fruit as it does among you, and has done since the day when you heard of the graciousness of God and recognized it for what in truth it is. You were taught this by Epa- 7 phras, our dear fellow-servant, a trusted worker for Christ on our behalf, and it is he who has brought us 8 the news of your God-given love.

✻ Thanksgiving often occupies the first part of Paul's letters.

3–4. God is described as *the Father of our Lord Jesus Christ* because Jesus in his earthly life claimed to be in a special relationship to God, referring to him as 'my Father'. After the resurrection of Jesus, his followers saw this claim to be true (see on Eph. 1: 3).

Thanksgiving, an important part of prayer, is an expression of gratitude to God for all his goodness. *faith,* i.e.

commitment and loyalty to Jesus, must result in *love*. This has as its pattern the generous love of God seen in Jesus, which is freely given without regard to return (Rom. 5: 8, 'but Christ died for us while we were yet sinners, and that is God's own proof of his love towards us').

5. The *faith* and *love* mentioned have point, because for Christians there is the *hope* that God and his cause will win the day; it will be shown that such *faith* and *love* are the things that really matter. *stored up in heaven* means that the hope is sure, because it is guaranteed by God and particularly by the resurrection of Jesus Christ. It is not, therefore, wishful thinking and hoping vaguely for something to turn up (see also above, p. 62).

6. The *Gospel* is *true*, as opposed to the other false theories about the world that were competing for the Colossians' allegiance. The extension and growing influence of the Gospel *to men the whole world over* shows its power. The Acts of the Apostles, while stressing that the Gospel is for the whole world, describes only the main outlines of the early Church's growth. But in its description of the spread of the Gospel from Jerusalem to Rome it leaves the powerful impression of the Church marching on against all the odds, and possessing a power that nothing can stop. *the day when you heard* was probably during Paul's activity at Ephesus (Acts 19: see above, p. 112). *the graciousness of God* is God's loving approach to us in Jesus Christ. Paul often uses this term *graciousness* or 'grace' to underline that our right relationship with God is not something due to our efforts (e.g. Rom. 3: 24, 'and all are justified by God's free grace alone').

7. *Epaphras* is also mentioned in Col. 4: 12 and Philem. 23. He came from Colossae, and is someone very much trusted by Paul. The name could be a shortened form of Epaphroditus. The latter is the name of a 'fellow-worker' of Paul (Phil. 2: 25). We cannot be sure that he and Epaphras are the same person. If *on our behalf* is the correct reading,

then we have the picture of the apostle with assistants working under his leadership. There is another reading mentioned
in the N.E.B. footnote: 'on your behalf'.

8. *brought us*, i.e. to Rome, according to the usual view.
God-given love (Greek: 'love in the Spirit'), i.e. a love fanned
into flame by the Holy Spirit of God. In other words, this
costly and generous love to others is a response to God's love,
needing his power to bring it to life.   ✻

THE PRAYER OF PAUL

For this reason, ever since the day we heard of it, we 9
have not ceased to pray for you. We ask God that you
may receive from him all wisdom and spiritual understanding for full insight into his will, so that your manner 10
of life may be worthy of the Lord and entirely pleasing
to him. We pray that you may bear fruit in active
goodness of every kind, and grow in the knowledge of
God. May he strengthen you, in his glorious might, with 11
ample power to meet whatever comes with fortitude,
patience, and joy; and to give thanks to the Father who 12
has made you fit to share the heritage of God's people
in the realm of light.

✻ Paul assures the Colossians that they are mentioned in his
prayers to God. The object of these prayers is that they may
plumb more and more the depths of the Gospel of Jesus and
all that it has to offer. For this section see also Eph. 1: 15–18.

9. Intercession—prayer for others—is one of the ways in
which the Christian co-operates with God. For the importance of prayer in the thought of Jesus and the early Church
see above, p. 40.

10. The Christian life is not something 'static', but a growth
in *insight* into how the mind and attitude of God revealed

in Jesus affect our present situation. *worthy of the Lord*, i.e. showing the qualities seen in the earthly life of Jesus. The use of the term *the Lord* is a reminder of the allegiance that the Christian owes to Jesus (see on Eph. 1: 2). Out of the Colossians' newly found relationship with God must result *active goodness*, i.e. the helping of others (see also the saying of Jesus, Mark 9: 35, 'If anyone wants to be first, he must make himself last of all and servant of all'). While Paul stresses that we cannot *earn* our friendship with God by our good deeds, yet he makes it clear that out of our love and loyalty for him these must follow. *knowledge of God* is not just knowing that he exists, but obedience to his will. Perhaps Paul stresses this because the other rival religions that were challenging the attention of the Colossians did not make such a close connection between religion and moral duty.

11. As Paul knew, loyalty to Jesus could bring with it all kinds of difficulties (*whatever comes*). Jesus too had clearly warned his disciples, 'All will hate you for your allegiance to me' (Mark 13: 13). But God, who had given a sign of his power in raising Jesus from the dead, could provide *ample power* to meet these trials with *fortitude*, *patience* (or better 'endurance'), and *joy*. Such *joy* comes from knowing that these sufferings are in the right cause of God, who in the person of Jesus Christ has himself suffered to restore human beings to himself (1 Pet. 3: 18, 'He [Jesus], the just, suffered for the unjust, to bring us to God'). Paul includes this joy among the important qualities of the Christian life (Gal. 5: 22, 'But the harvest of the Spirit is love, joy, peace...').

12. Thanksgiving—the continual remembering of what is owed to God—gives balance to the Christian life. *the heritage* in the Old Testament describes the blessing of the land of Canaan (Deut. 15: 4, '...the land which the Lord thy God giveth thee for an inheritance to possess it'). It is now used of the status of those who are reconciled and put right with God in Jesus. *made you fit* stresses that the status is purely due to the grace of God. *in the realm of light*, because Jesus is 'the

light of the world' (John 8: 12), and because those who belong to him share in the light that he brings of God's purposes and nature. Therefore Christians could describe themselves as 'children of light' (1 Thess. 5: 4), or as 'men who are at home in daylight' (Eph. 5: 8). Jesus too had said to his disciples, 'You are light for all the world' (Matt. 5: 14). For the Jewish sect at Qumran as 'the sons of light', see above, p. 93. *

JESUS THE SOURCE OF ALL EXISTENCE

He rescued us from the domain of darkness and brought 13 us away into the kingdom of his dear Son, in whom 14 our release is secured and our sins forgiven. He is the 15 image of the invisible God; his is the primacy over all created things. In him everything in heaven and on 16 earth was created, not only things visible but also the invisible orders of thrones, sovereignties, authorities, and powers; the whole universe has been created through him and for him. And he exists before everything, and 17 all things are held together in him.

* Here and in the following section we have a description of the person and status of Jesus by whom God's 'rescue operation' is carried out. Several points are worth noting: (i) the description of Jesus in 1: 15–20 may be based on a creed or hymn well known to the Colossians, (ii) a parallel is drawn between the work of Jesus in creation (verses 15–17) and his part in reclaiming God's world (verses 18–20), and it is because of the first of these activities that Jesus can perform the second, (iii) the fact that the early disciples of Jesus could, after his resurrection, give him the high status described here shows what a tremendous impression he had made upon them, (iv) all through the passage Jesus is seen as the source and

origin of *all created things* and the point where men are confronted with God. This emphasis is probably aimed at the propaganda in Colossae that was trying to destroy the uniqueness of Jesus.

13. *the domain of darkness* is a way of describing those who are out of touch with God and are opposed to or ignorant of what he stands for. The Jews believed that God would act to challenge this darkness with his 'light' and to claim back men's allegiance. The Christians believed that this 'confrontation' had taken place in the mission and work of Jesus (John 3: 19, 'Here lies the test: the light has come into the world, but men preferred darkness to light...'). He had established a kingdom of those who accepted God as the centre of their lives. *his dear Son*: a description of the unique relationship between Jesus and God (see above on Eph. 4: 13).

14. *release* (a term taken from the giving of liberty to slaves) was offered by many religions of Paul's day. They held out the hope of freedom from the trammels of the earthly body, and of securing immortality. Besides freedom from fear, an important element in the *release* promised by Jesus is the assurance that God forgives our disobedience and gives a new start. Jesus claimed authority in his earthly ministry to bring the assurance of God's forgiveness, e.g. to the paralysed man (Mark 2: 5, 'My son, your sins are forgiven'). He also commissioned his disciples to do the same (Luke 24: 47, 'and that in his name repentance bringing the forgiveness of sins is to be proclaimed to all nations'). This knowledge of God's forgiveness can bring freedom from those feelings of guilt which lie at the bottom of some mental disorders.

15. *the image of...God.* Jesus is here described as the 'Word' or 'Wisdom' of God through which God was believed in Jewish thought to have created the world and to maintain contact with it. The early Christians' experience of Jesus Christ as mediator between God and themselves led them to equate him with this Word or Wisdom (see above, p. 109).

16. *heaven* is here a way of describing the invisible part of the universe, and *everything in heaven* describes superhuman forces of evil at work against God. These malignant forces are trying to rival God and keep him from his proper place (see also above, p. 36). They are further described in what follows. In Paul's time there was a common belief in *invisible orders* of angels and superhuman forces, which were sometimes thought to inhabit the planets and have an important say in man's destiny. These powers described as *the invisible orders of thrones* etc. often exercised an unhealthy fear on people's minds. Paul may here be quoting the terms used to describe these powers in the propaganda of the rival Mystery religions. In the cult of Mithra, already mentioned, p. 25, the seven planets and the twelve signs of the Zodiac were regarded as divine beings, exercising potent influences for good or evil upon human destiny. It was thought that each of these planets presided over a day of the week. If these forces exist, says Paul, they must be seen in their right perspective as part of the created order, and so subordinate to Jesus Christ. Too often through human credulity and fear they have wrongly exercised a power and influence due to God alone. *For him*: the sole purpose of the universe is to serve the glory of the one true God.

17. *held together*. Through Jesus Christ, his Word, God is continually at work in his world; it is not the case that he created it and then left it to its own devices. ✷

JESUS THE RESTORER

He is, moreover, the head of the body, the Church. He 18 is its origin, the first to return from the dead, to be in all things alone supreme. For in him the complete being 19 of God, by God's own choice, came to dwell. Through 20 him God chose to reconcile the whole universe to himself, making peace through the shedding of his blood upon the cross—to reconcile all things, whether on earth or in heaven, through him alone.

✳ Jesus Christ is not only the source of creation but the one who creates order out of the disorder that has crept into God's universe and is reflected partly in the disobedience of human beings to God's will.

18. The order that Jesus brings is to be observed in *the church*, the family of those who recognize the demands of God. For the word *church* see on Eph. I: 22. *The head* and *the body* describe 'the ruler' and 'the sphere ruled over' (see above, p. III). What brought the community of Jesus, the church, into being as an effective force in the world was the conviction of his disciples that after his crucifixion Jesus was not finished but was still the great factor for their own lives and for the world. He is therefore *its origin*, because he is *the first to return from the dead*. Death (even if merely regarded as a natural phenomenon) spells out the message of the purposelessness of human life, and in Paul's time also symbolized the power of evil. Jesus is the only one in the world's history who has convincingly shown that death did not put an end to his career, and so he is *alone supreme*, the centre of human hopes and aspirations.

19. In the Old Testament we are told that it was God's *choice* to *dwell* in the Jewish Temple (Ps. 68: 16, 'Why look ye askance, ye high mountains, At the mountain which God hath desired for his abode?'). Now he meets with men in the human being Jesus of Nazareth. Here and nowhere else is *the complete being of God*, i.e. his true nature and character, to be found (see also on 2: 9). For this reason Jesus claims our attention for the understanding of human life.

20. God and his world are at 'loggerheads' and Jesus is the 'reconciliation officer' to bring the two parties together. But the role of peacemaker can be costly and it leads to Jesus' death by crucifixion in which God's love is revealed and his right hand of friendship is held out: see also above, p. 35.

whether on earth or in heaven stresses that God's act of reconciliation concerns all beings, human and others (see on 1: 16).
alone: once more it is stressed that Jesus is the only 'Saviour',
the only means by which we come to terms with the world
in which we live. ✷

THE CHANGED SITUATION

Formerly you were yourselves estranged from God; you 21
were his enemies in heart and mind, and your deeds were
evil. But now by Christ's death in his body of flesh and 22
blood God has reconciled you to himself, so that he may
present you before himself as dedicated men, without
blemish and innocent in his sight. Only you must 23
continue in your faith, firm on your foundations, never
to be dislodged from the hope offered in the gospel
which you heard. This is the gospel which has been
proclaimed in the whole creation under heaven; and I,
Paul, have become its minister.

✷ The new status and prospects of the Colossians are now
described.

21. The Colossians had worshipped false gods and had
conformed to the prevalent standards of conduct of the pagan
world. They were *enemies in heart and mind*, because their
attitudes and wishes were opposed to those of God, and
resulted naturally in actions or *deeds* that were *evil.*

22. *body of flesh and blood* stresses that God's act of reconciliation was done not by remote control but right in the
midst of human life (see also Gal. 4: 4, 'God sent his own
Son, born of a woman...').

present: God is perhaps seen here as a King having people
presented to him at court.

dedicated, i.e. fully committed to God's cause.

without blemish and innocent, i.e. obedient to God and so without guilt (see also on Eph. 5: 25–27).

23. *faith*: probably here the belief that in Jesus Christ God gives the key to his purposes, which forms a true *foundation* for life.

hope, i.e. that God's cause will win the day, and that he has a place for us in his purposes.

in the whole creation under heaven must refer partly to the wide extent of the Church's preaching, though, if used of the Church's preaching alone, the phrase seems exaggerated. Shortly before this time Paul claims to have preached the Gospel from Jerusalem to Illyricum (Romans 15: 19, 'As a result I have completed the preaching of the gospel of Christ from Jerusalem as far round as Illyricum'). He had *become its minister*, i.e. he had been specially commissioned as an apostle, which he traced to the experience described in Acts 9: 1–19 and referred to in Gal. 1: 15–17, 'But then in his good pleasure God...chose to reveal his Son to me and through me that I might proclaim him among the Gentiles.' For *minister* see on Eph. 3: 7. He was one among many evangelists. Paul may also mean that the news about Jesus Christ has spread even where the Church's evangelists have not been. But he may imply, too, that apart from human agency the Gospel has had repercussions on the whole world. ✶

THE PURPOSE OF PAUL'S MINISTRY

24 It is now my happiness to suffer for you. This is my way of helping to complete, in my poor human flesh, the full tale of Christ's afflictions still to be endured, for the
25 sake of his body which is the church. I became its servant
26 by virtue of the task assigned to me by God for your benefit: to deliver his message in full; to announce the secret hidden for long ages and through many genera-

tions, but now disclosed to God's people, to whom it 27 was his will to make it known—to make known how rich and glorious it is among all nations. The secret is this: Christ in you, the hope of a glory to come.

✴ Paul now speaks of the purpose of his sufferings, and of the secret that it is his task to proclaim. The present section should be compared with Eph. 3: 1–13.

24. Paul even sees that his present sufferings as a prisoner are not just frustrating, but somehow have a place in God's plans. Rather mysteriously, Paul believes that before God's Kingdom comes there is a full *tale* or quota of suffering to be paid. This quota of *Christ's afflictions* includes Jesus' own sufferings in his earthly life but also what he continues to suffer in the person of his followers, the Church. Paul sees his troubles as helping to make up the quota and so bringing nearer the time when the Church and what it stands for will be vindicated. For the connection between *happiness* and suffering, see Matt. 5: 11, 'How blest you are, when you suffer insults and persecution and every kind of calumny for my sake. Accept it with gladness and exaltation...'

25. *the message*: of God's love spoken in Jesus Christ and the assurance that God is King and will work his purposes.

26. *the secret*, or 'mystery'. In the world of Paul's time there were many societies claiming to give secret teaching on the meaning of life, which was revealed only to members. Christianity is an open secret offered openly to everyone. It is only a *secret* in the sense that God's plan for restoring human beings to himself was kept secret until the right time arrived (*now*). *God's people*, i.e. the Church, which possesses this open secret to pass on to others. For God's choice of the right moment see on Eph. 1: 10.

27. The gospel is so *rich* and *glorious*, i.e. so full of potentialities for human life, that it must be made known to all. In other words, as we saw above, p. 126, Christianity has a world-wide coverage. Paul speaks of the Christians' union

with Jesus Christ in two ways, as their being 'in Christ' (e.g. 1: 2), and of Christ being in them (as here *in you*), just as branches grafted into a tree draw on the tree's life. This 'link-up' with Jesus Christ assures us that we are in tune with God here and now, and gives *the hope* of a fuller life with God, with which physical death cannot interfere. This fuller life is in the New Testament connected with the final triumph of God over all that opposes him, as below in 3: 4, 'When Christ, who is our life, is manifested, then you too will be manifested with him in glory' (see also 'Christian prospects', p. 125). ✶

PAUL'S CONCERN FOR THE CHRISTIAN CHURCHES

28 He it is whom we proclaim. We admonish everyone without distinction, we instruct everyone in all the ways of wisdom, so as to present each one of you as a mature
29 member of Christ's body. To this end I am toiling strenuously with all the energy and power of Christ at
2 work in me. For I want you to know how strenuous are my exertions for you and the Laodiceans and all who
2 have never set eyes on me. I want them to continue in good heart and in the unity of love, and to come to the full wealth of conviction which understanding brings,
3 and grasp God's secret. That secret is Christ himself; in him lie hidden all God's treasures of wisdom and know-
4 ledge. I tell you this to save you from being talked into
5 error by specious arguments. For though absent in body, I am with you in spirit, and rejoice to see your orderly array and the firm front which your faith in Christ presents.

✶ Although he does not know its members personally, Paul assures the Church at Colossae of his anxiety for their welfare.

28. *He it is*, aimed perhaps at those who were trying to combine Jesus Christ with other schemes of salvation. The stress on *everyone* and *all the ways* may be due to the existence of other sects and religions that confined their teaching to the privileged few. Paul's aim is that the Colossians should be *mature* or 'grown up', i.e. understanding and living out the full implications of the Gospel of Jesus Christ, and playing their full part in *Christ's body*, the Church. For *present* see above on 1: 22.

29. Even in prison Paul is not just sitting back, but is busy directing missionary operations. Yet he takes no credit for this activity, as his energy is Christ-given and not his own.

2: 1-2. Laodicea (see above, p. 112) was a city some distance east of Ephesus and part of the Roman Province of Asia (see map, p. ix). It was situated on the river Lycus. The Christians at Colossae and Laodicea had not *set eyes* on Paul, for the churches in this area had not been founded through personal visits of Paul (see above, p. 112). The basis of *unity* in a Christian congregation must be *love* of the generous kind seen in Jesus Christ. The Christian is not called to a blind faith in God, but comes to *conviction* by *understanding*, i.e. by seeing the reasonable historical evidence on which such faith is based and the reasonable solution to life that it gives. *grasp* is 'to realize the full implications of'.

3. God's nature and purposes are an open *secret* in Jesus Christ. Again it is stressed that everything one needs to know about God is found in him. Paul is thinking of those who wish to fit the Gospel into other schemes for coming to terms with life. *hidden*, i.e. like treasure waiting to be dug up.

4. the *error* of denying the uniqueness of Jesus Christ. *specious arguments*, e.g. that it is safer to combine elements in different religions and so take out a comprehensive policy for securing one's destiny (see above, p. 121).

5. *in spirit*: in the sense that Paul feels himself involved with the Colossians in all that concerns them, and is united with them in his prayers. *orderly array* and *firm front* are

probably military terms, describing an army keeping its tidy formation under pressure. *faith in Christ*, i.e. loyalty to him. ✳

THE DANGER OF BEING SIDETRACKED

6 Therefore, since Jesus was delivered to you as Christ
7 and Lord, live your lives in union with him. Be rooted in him; be built in him; be consolidated in the faith you were taught; let your hearts overflow with thankfulness.
8 Be on your guard; do not let your minds be captured by hollow and delusive speculations, based on traditions of man-made teaching and centred on the elemental spirits of the world and not on Christ.

✳ Once more it is stressed that Jesus is the only centre of the Christian life. Speculations about the planetary powers and their effect on human destiny are not to be heeded.

6. *delivered* has to do with the passing on of a tradition. Paul several times refers to the common tradition about Jesus that he has received from the church (e.g. 1 Cor. 15: 3, 'First and foremost, I handed on to you the facts which had been imparted to me: that Christ died for our sins, in accordance with the scriptures; that he was buried; that he was raised to life on the third day, according to the scriptures'). A more literal translation would be: 'since you received the tradition of the Anointed King, Jesus, the Lord'. *Christ* is here a title describing Jesus as King, and like the word *Lord* describes the claim of Jesus on human allegiance. For *Christ* and *Lord* see on Eph. 1: 2.

7. *rooted, built, consolidated*—all stress that Jesus Christ must be the pivot of the life of the Colossian Church. *faith*: here probably the belief that 'God was in Christ [and in him alone] reconciling the world to himself' (2 Cor. 5: 19). *taught*, i.e. when they were instructed by Epaphras and others

in the meaning of the faith, prior to their baptism. *thankful-ness*, with its reminder of God's mercies, will be a further support.

8. In the first century A.D. there were a lot of *speculations* about the divine powers that controlled the universe and about the correct way of coming to terms with them. This discussion was often based on old myths or legends about gods or goddesses. Its basis was therefore *man-made* as opposed to Christianity which is solidly based on a historical character, Jesus Christ, and on convincing evidence of his importance as the one in whom God speaks to man. In these *speculations* the *elemental spirits* or powers that were thought to inhabit the planets loomed large (see above on 1: 16). The word translated here as *elemental spirits* could mean the funda-mental principles of knowledge; it was also applied to the basic elements that made up the natural world (i.e. earth, air, fire and water) which were sometimes thought of as spirit powers. But the term was also used, as here, of the 'heavenly bodies' and the powers that were thought to dwell in them. These were considered to have an influence on human affairs, just as people today believe in fate and read their horoscopes in the daily papers, and sometimes take them seriously. ✳

THE ONE WAY TO LIFE

For it is in Christ that the complete being of the Godhead 9
dwells embodied, and in him you have been brought to 10
completion. Every power and authority in the universe
is subject to him as Head. In him also you were circum- 11
cised, not in a physical sense, but by being divested of
the lower nature; this is Christ's way of circumcision.
For in baptism you were buried with him, in baptism 12
also you were raised to life with him through your faith
in the active power of God who raised him from the

13 dead. And although you were dead because of your sins and because you were morally uncircumcised, he has made you alive with Christ. For he has forgiven us all
14 our sins; he has cancelled the bond which pledged us to the decrees of the law. It stood against us, but he has set
15 it aside, nailing it to the cross. On that cross he discarded the cosmic powers and authorities like a garment; he made a public spectacle of them and led them as captives in his triumphal procession.

✴ Paul now describes what the Colossians owe to Jesus.

9. *embodied* stresses the fact that in this human quest for the divine controllers of the universe, the one and only divine power that matters confronts us in the life, death, resurrection and present lordship of Jesus. *Godhead* was used in Paul's time of the divine quality that was thought to be shared among a large number of superhuman beings and gods. It was even sometimes attributed to human beings (e.g. the Roman emperors). But for Paul, who had been brought up a Jew, there is only the one God who possesses this divine quality (Eph. 4: 6, 'one God and Father of all, who is over all and through all and in all'). Jesus, as God's Word, shares in this quality, and the same applies to the Holy Spirit.

10. *completion*, i.e. to a complete understanding of the meaning of the universe. Jesus' lordship over *every power and authority* has already been stressed in 1: 16. Such powers and authorities were ways of describing superhuman forces of evil, which were thought to hold a grip over human lives. For Jesus' defeat of these powers see on 2: 15.

11. Physical *circumcision* or removal of the foreskin was performed upon all male Jews eight days after birth. This was a sign of their membership of God's people (Gen. 17: 10, 'This is my covenant which ye shall keep, between me and you and thy seed after thee; every male among you shall be circumcised'). But in the best Jewish teaching it was seen

as only the outward sign of 'the circumcision of the heart', i.e. the removal of all that prevents complete loyalty to God (see e.g. Deut. 10: 16, 'Circumcise therefore the foreskin of your heart, and be no more stiffnecked'). Christian baptism could therefore easily be described as a *circumcision*, the removal not just of something physical, but of *the lower nature* (Greek: 'the body of the flesh'), i.e. a self-centredness that is blind to the demands of God and needs of others. Paul, as here, frequently uses the word 'flesh' (usually translated in the N.E.B. as 'the lower nature') to describe the impulse in human beings that pulls them away from God (e.g. Gal. 5: 19, 'Anyone can see the kind of behaviour that belongs to the lower nature').

12. The act of *burial* of the physical body at death means the abrupt end to life on earth. So the immersion beneath the water at baptism means a decisive death to self-living. But the burial of Jesus Christ marks also the completion of an earthly life characterized by obedience to and trust in God. Burial *with him* means the association of oneself with that way of life. But just as through *the active power of God* Jesus despite his death came back to be a living and powerful force in the world, so in baptism the Christian is *raised*, i.e. linked to that source of power, and committed to live at the level demanded by Jesus. This 'resurrection' was symbolized by the candidate's coming up from the water after his immersion. But if such baptism is to be effective, it must be accompanied by the firm conviction or *faith* that God can help us to live at this higher level of life (see also 'Christian security' above, p. 124).

13. *sins*, because they are acts of disobedience to God, create a gulf between him and human beings, and so cause *death*, because the purpose of human life is obedience to God. *morally uncircumcised* (Greek: 'with uncircumcision of the flesh'), i.e. with unrestrained self-interest. *made alive*, i.e. brought them to the true purpose of life, obedience to God, with the power to live it. To be *made alive* means also that

God has *forgiven us all our sins.* Jesus in his earthly ministry brought the assurance of God's forgiveness and the offer of a new start in the face of human *sins* and disobedience to God. Similarly *the cross* mentioned in verse 15 below speaks of God's love and forgiveness (see also 1: 14).

14. *bond...law* (Greek: 'the certificate of debt with its ordinances'). These *ordinances* were for the Jews (as the N.E.B. suggests) the Old Testament Law, described at Eph. 2: 15. For the pagan Colossians they were the regulations required to keep the favour of their gods, e.g. the rules mentioned in 2: 21. In both cases there was the sense of being in debt and never 'catching up with one's payments'. Such an approach to God and other divine powers, built on the keeping of minute regulations, necessarily led to a feeling that one was not carrying out all that was required, and so to fear and tension. God has, however, *cancelled the bond* of debt. First, he has shown in Jesus that the relationship of human beings to himself is based on love, and not on an idea that God is the creditor and we are the debtors. Secondly, God has shown that the 'cosmic powers and authorities' are not to be feared and therefore regulations to keep on the right side of them are idle (see verse 15). *Nailing*: a bond of debt was sometimes cancelled by driving a nail through it and placing it on the debtor's door.

15. The general picture is that of a Roman general entering Rome in triumph after a great victory. This was a privilege only granted in this period to members of the emperor's family. In such a triumph the prisoners taken in the war would be displayed as part of the procession. *discarded like a garment* could also be translated 'disarmed', which would fit in with the general picture. But the Greek word here is closely connected with the word *divested* in verse 11 above. Christians can be 'divested of the lower nature' in baptism, because Jesus *discarded* the *cosmic powers and authorities* like a garment for which he had no use. Jesus was obedient to God even when it meant dying the death of crucifixion, a death

reserved for the worst criminals, and believed by the Jews to denote God's curse (Deut. 21: 22–3). In this way God defeated the *cosmic powers and authorities*, and took them captive. The latter are the forces at work against God, which prey on 'the lower nature' and would have pulled Jesus in the direction of selfishness and of saving his own life. We may think of these forces as standing for men's fears of various kinds. They were defeated by Jesus' committal of himself in complete trust to God both in his life and in the face of a death unjustly inflicted on him.   *

THE WRONG RECIPE

Allow no one therefore to take you to task about what 16 you eat or drink, or over the observance of festival, new moon, or sabbath. These are no more than a shadow 17 of what was to come; the solid reality is Christ's. You 18 are not to be disqualified by the decision of people who go in for self-mortification and angel-worship, and try to enter into some vision of their own. Such people, bursting with the futile conceit of worldly minds, lose 19 hold upon the Head; yet it is from the Head that the whole body, with all its joints and ligaments, receives its supplies, and thus knit together grows according to God's design.

* We see something here of the rival scheme of 'salvation' that is being put before the Colossian Christians.

16. These regulation sound like Jewish laws of the Old Testament. The all-inclusive scheme of 'salvation' being put forward may have included observance of parts of the Old Testament Law (see above, pp. 118–20). *what you eat or drink* is reminiscent of Jewish rules about distinguishing between what is unclean and clean (e.g. Lev. 11: 47, 'to make a difference between the unclean and the clean, and

between the living thing that may be eaten and the living thing that may not be eaten'). Similarly, the *observance of festival, new moon, or sabbath* is referred to e.g. in Ezek. 45: 17, 'And it shall be the prince's part to give the burnt offerings, and the meal offerings, and the drink offerings, in the feasts and in the new moons, and in the sabbaths.' The festivals included the celebration of the Passover feast (see e.g. Exod. 12: 1–20). The keeping of the Sabbath or seventh day of the week was a leading feature of the Jewish religion (Exod. 20: 10, 'but the seventh day is a sabbath unto the Lord thy God: in it thou shalt not do any work...').

17. These regulations formed the basis of Jewish loyalty to God and so prepared the way for his greater revelation of himself in Jesus (*the solid reality*).

18. *disqualified*: used of an umpire in games giving a decision against someone. In this case the prize lost is the key to the universe and life. These obscure practices appear to be aimed at keeping right with the planetary powers. They involved ascetic practices and rites, which were supposed to give special knowledge, see also above, p. 120. *futile conceit*, i.e. of believing that they could discover the true meaning of life by their own efforts.

19. *body* is sometimes interpreted as 'the universe' which finds its centre of direction in Jesus. More likely, however, this verse is to be seen in the light of 1: 18, where *the body* is the Church. Jesus is the sole source of its life and growth and admits of no rival partners. For this description of *the body*, see on Eph. 4: 16, and for the use of *the Head* and *the body* see above, p. 110. ✳

CHRISTIAN FREEDOM

20 Did you not die with Christ and pass beyond reach of the elemental spirits of the world? Then why behave as though you were still living the life of the world? Why
21 let people dictate to you: 'Do not handle this, do not

taste that, do not touch the other'—all of them things ₂₂ that must perish as soon as they are used? That is to follow merely human injunctions and teaching. True, ₂₃ it has an air of wisdom, with its forced piety, its self-mortification, and its severity to the body; but it is of no use at all in combating sensuality.

Were you not raised to life with Christ? Then aspire **3** to the realm above, where Christ is, seated at the right hand of God, and let your thoughts dwell on that higher ₂ realm, not on this earthly life. I repeat, you died; and ₃ now your life lies hidden with Christ in God. When ₄ Christ, who is our life, is manifested, then you too will be manifested with him in glory.

---

* The Colossian Christians are not to see themselves as set in a hostile world, at the mercy of malignant forces which are to be won over at any cost.

20. In his readiness and willingness to face death Jesus subscribed to the view of life which says: 'At the heart of the world is not something cold, heartless and hostile, but something warm, the God of love, whose cause will prevail.' To *die with Christ* is to make the same act of faith which removes fears that one's destiny is controlled by evil spirits and powers. Paul thinks of this death as taking place in baptism; see above on 2: 12. *The life of the world* is the life dogged by fears and dreads and by the feeling that everything is against one.

21–22. Perhaps all these practices were being recommended as suitable for keeping on the right side of the forces of evil. To be obsessed by the need to abstain from this or that makes material things loom far larger than they should.

23. Such self-imposed disciplines may seem to have *an air of wisdom* and appear very valuable, but may encourage self-reliance rather than reliance on God in fighting *sensuality*, i.e. the pull that is in all of us against the will and demands

of God. Paul knew the weakness of the human will (Rom. 7: 19, 'The good which I want to do, I fail to do; but what I do is the wrong which is against my will').

3: 1–2. God set the seal of his approval on Jesus by raising him from the dead. He therefore showed that the viewpoint of Jesus on human life was correct, i.e., that trust in the loving God and obedience to his will are the stuff of life. To be *raised to life with Christ* is to accept and share in this higher plane of life, which Jesus, now enthroned as King, embodies and represents. This is what is meant by *aspiring to the realm above* and by letting *your thoughts dwell on that higher realm*.

seated at the right hand of God describes (*a*) God's vindication of Jesus' mission, (*b*) his enthronement as King of the world, (*c*) Jesus' return to his heavenly glory, after his earthly mission is completed (for the language see Psalm 110: 1, 'The Lord says to my lord: "Sit at my right hand..."' R.S.V.). Jesus had used this language of the status of the expected Jewish Messiah or King (Mark 12: 35–37) and had in this way also described his confidence that God would vindicate his own mission (Mark 14: 62, '...and you will see the Son of Man seated on the right hand of God'). *not on this earthly life*: Paul is not saying that our present life on earth and our material things do not matter, but rather that they need to be seen against the background of God's purposes.

3–4. *died*. See on 2: 20. Jesus' kingship is *hidden* in the sense that it has not been finally and openly demonstrated. In the same way the Christian attitude to life lies *hidden* because it has not yet been fully demonstrated as the true way of life. But in the future Jesus will be *manifested*, i.e. shown as the undisputed King of the world, and the rightness of the Christian interpretation of life demonstrated. It is Jesus' resurrection that gives Paul this confidence that Christians will be shown to have staked their all in the right cause. To be *manifested...in glory* is a way of describing the full life with God that awaits Christians when God's plans for the world have been achieved. ✷

LIFE ON THE HIGHER PLANE

Then put to death those parts of you which belong to 5
the earth—fornication, indecency, lust, foul cravings, and
the ruthless greed which is nothing less than idolatry.
Because of these, God's dreadful judgement is impending; 6
and in the life you once lived these are the ways you 7
yourselves followed. But now you yourselves must lay 8
aside all anger, passion, malice, cursing, filthy talk—have
done with them! Stop lying to one another, now that 9
you have discarded the old nature with its deeds and have 10
put on the new nature, which is being constantly renewed in the image of its Creator and brought to know
God. There is no question here of Greek and Jew, 11
circumcised and uncircumcised, barbarian, Scythian,
freeman, slave; but Christ is all, and is in all.

✳ Paul describes the consequences of living on the higher
level demanded by Jesus. This section should be compared
with Eph. 4: 31 — 5: 5.

5. To 'die with Christ', as already described at 2: 20,
brings with it the need to *put to death those parts of you that
belong to the earth*, i.e. what is self-centred. In this way to die
with Jesus is something continually going on. The first three
vices—*fornication, indecency, lust*—all concern the selfish use
of sex for one's own ends. The last two have to do with a
selfish desire to satisfy one's own wants, right or wrong, whoever suffers in the process. *idolatry*, because 'self' can be the
worst of false gods.

6. *God's judgement* (Greek: 'the wrath of God') is seen partly
in the disintegration and distress caused in human life by self-
interest, and partly in the fact that God will finally make clear
his condemnation of such selfishness. For 'the wrath of God'
see also on Eph. 2: 3.

8. The *now* is emphatic. Committal to Jesus is to have an immediate effect on one's behaviour. *lay aside* is thought to have been a set formula used in the moral teaching of the early Church (see also Eph. 4: 22, 25). Here it is closely linked with verse 9 which follows: 'now that you have discarded the old nature'. *anger* and *passion* can be of a righteous kind, but are often due to a selfish feeling of being thwarted in some way. *malice*, the desire to hurt another, and *cursing*, one of the expressions of it, both contradict the Christian attitude of love. Jesus himself warned of the dangers of *talk* or the tongue as revealing the man's real self (Matt. 12: 34). See also above, p. 75.

9. *lying* includes unfaithfulness and deception. Appeal is made to the Colossians' baptism in which they discarded one kind of life for another. The *old nature* (Greek: 'the old man') stands for all that we have in common with Adam, who in the story of Gen. 3 represents the person who makes 'self' his god, and whose *deeds* will also be selfish.

10. The *new nature* (Greek: 'the new man') is the character and quality of life seen in Jesus. It is being *constantly renewed* in the sense that the Colossians have accepted this way of life as that into which they must grow. In Gen. 1: 26, man is said to have been made *in the image of* God, i.e. capable of entering into a personal relationship with his maker and of knowing him, i.e. obeying him.

11. The various terms used here are a way of referring to the national, religious, social and racial distinctions in the ancient world. Paul starts with the distinction, in the world of Roman civilization, between *Jew* and *Greek* (a way of speaking of the non-Jew, and not merely of someone who came from Greece). Circumcision was the mark of the Jew (see above on 2: 11). Paul passes to the *barbarian* and *Scythian*, which were derogatory terms for the peoples outside the culture and civilization of the Roman world. There is also the big social cleavage between *freeman* and *slave* (see also below on 3: 22–25). But Jesus Christ is *all and in all* in the sense that he forms a

whole in which all these divisions can be included (see also
Gal. 3: 28 and Eph. 2: 11–22). ✴

THE QUALITIES OF THE CHRISTIAN LIFE

Then put on the garments that suit God's chosen people,   12
his own, his beloved: compassion, kindness, humility,
gentleness, patience. Be forbearing with one another,   13
and forgiving, where any of you has cause for complaint:
you must forgive as the Lord forgave you. To crown   14
all, there must be love, to bind all together and complete
the whole. Let Christ's peace be arbiter in your hearts: 15
to this peace you were called as members of a single
body. And be filled with gratitude. Let the message of   16
Christ dwell among you in all its richness. Instruct and
admonish each other with the utmost wisdom. Sing
thankfully in your hearts to God, with psalms and hymns
and spiritual songs. Whatever you are doing, whether   17
you speak or act, do everything in the name of the Lord
Jesus, giving thanks to God the Father through him.

✴ Paul now lists some of the qualities and characteristics that
make up the 'new nature' mentioned in 3: 10. These qualities
are important, because they marked the earthly life of Jesus.
Some of the other driving forces behind the Christian life are
also mentioned, e.g. thanksgiving. This section should be
compared with Eph. 4: 2; 4: 32 — 5: 2; and 5: 19–20.

12. *God's chosen people, his own, his beloved* describes the
status and privileges of Christians, and underlines the necessity
of living a life worthy of them. *chosen* stresses the belief of the
early Christians that (*a*) they owed their new relationship to
God purely to his goodness and not to any worthiness in
themselves and (*b*) they had a special part to play in God's
plans. *his own* is literally 'set apart', emphasizing that Christians

are committed to serve God. *beloved*, i.e. they are the recipients of the love of God seen in Jesus. *put on* is similarly used in Isa. 59: 17, 'And he put on righteousness as a breastplate...' *compassion* and *kindness* were prominent features of Jesus' dealings with people, e.g. with the woman that was 'living an immoral life' (Luke 7: 36–50). *humility* does not mean a cringing attitude and a false belittlement of self; it is to make a proper valuation of oneself, as being intended to be dependent on God and to serve him. *gentleness* should not suggest a timid refusal to stand up for one's convictions. It may be another way of talking of *humility*, or may be used here of courteous consideration for others. *patience* is a characteristic of God in the Old Testament, who is described as 'patient' or 'slow to anger' (e.g. Ps. 103: 8, 'The Lord is full of compassion and gracious, Slow to anger, and plenteous in mercy'). Here it means a refusal to be hasty with our fellow human beings, and an attempt to understand them and sympathize with them.

13. As with *patience*, so with *forbearing*, this is not just 'putting up' with someone by some means or other; it involves an understanding love, and a readiness to be *forgiving*. Forgiveness is a willingness to blot out *the cause for complaint* and start afresh as though it had never happened. *the Lord* is probably here a reference to Jesus, who brought to men the assurance of God's forgiveness (see above on 2: 13). Paul is probably thinking here of baptism, in and through which the Colossians had received the assurance that they were cleansed from their past sins, and were given a new start.

14. What gives the Christian life coherence is *love*, the costly and generous love seen in Jesus. The best comment on this verse is Paul's famous hymn to 'love' in 1 Cor. 13, where the theme is 'if I have no love, I am nothing' (verse 2).

15. *arbiter*: the word is used of an umpire to whom reference is made for decisions in the games. The umpire here is *Christ's peace*, i.e. the reconciliation that he has brought between God and man. This fact is the starting-point of reference for the living of one's whole life. The *single body*, the

Church, consists of those who have accepted this call of God in Jesus to be at one with him. A deep sense of *gratitude* to God for his approach to us can be a driving force behind the Christian life.

16. The *message of Christ* includes not only his words, but his actions, his death and resurrection. *the richness*—the full implication of all that Jesus said and did—has to be continually plumbed. In the understanding of the implications of the Gospel the different members of the church have all some *wisdom* or insight to contribute. As elsewhere Paul stresses that a Christian is not an isolated individual, but a member of a family where people learn from each other (see also 1 Cor. 14: 26, 'when you meet for worship, each of you contributes a hymn, some instruction, a revelation, an ecstatic utterance, or the interpretation of such an utterance'). Similarly gratitude to God is a 'together' activity which can indeed be conveyed in words of song but which should be the expression of something deeply felt. The use of *psalms* from the Old Testament probably had a place in the Church's worship from a very early time. The *hymns* and *spiritual songs* mentioned here were probably mainly Christian compositions, which may have included some of the songs preserved in the Revelation of John (e.g. 5: 9–10), as well as the 'Song of Mary' (Luke 1: 46) and the 'Song of Simeon' (Luke 2: 29).

17. *in the name of*, i.e. with proper respect to the honour of Jesus. All one's actions are to be the means of *giving thanks to God*, i.e. they are to be worthy of him, and so an expression of our gratitude for what he has done for us. *through him*, because it is in Jesus that God approaches us and summons us in turn to approach him. ✳

RELATIONSHIPS

Wives, be subject to your husbands: that is your Christian 18
duty. Husbands, love your wives and do not be harsh 19
with them. Children, obey your parents in everything, 20

for that is pleasing to God and is the Christian way.
21 Fathers, do not exasperate your children, for fear they
22 grow disheartened. Slaves, give entire obedience to your
earthly masters, not merely with an outward show of
service, to curry favour with men, but with single-
23 mindedness, out of reverence for the Lord. Whatever
you are doing, put your whole heart into it, as if you
24 were doing it for the Lord and not for men, knowing
that there is a Master who will give you your heritage
as a reward for your service. Christ is the Master whose
25 slaves you must be. Dishonesty will be requited, and he
4 has no favourites. Masters, be just and fair to your
slaves, knowing that you too have a Master in heaven.

* Advice is here given to various classes of people. A similar
scheme of instruction is found in Eph. 5: 22 — 6: 9; 1 Pet. 2:
13 — 3: 7, and may be based on a 'church catechism' or
manual of instruction which was used in the preparation of candidates for baptism, and which set out the duties of Christians.
Such a catechism may be referred to in Rom. 6: 17 ('But God
be thanked, you, who once were slaves of sin, have yielded
whole-hearted obedience to the pattern of teaching to which
you were made subject') and in 1 Thess. 4: 1 ('We passed on
to you the tradition of the way we must live to please God').
The Stoics, who were an important philosophical sect of the
period, and whose leading beliefs have already been discussed,
p. 20, had developed a moral code dealing with human relationships. For example, a prominent Stoic of the time was the
Roman author and politician, Seneca, who was an adviser of
the Emperor Nero (A.D. 54–68), a brother of Gallio, the
governor of Achaia (Acts 18: 12), and a contemporary of
Paul. He speaks of 'that part of philosophy which gives advice
suitable to each individual person, without its applying to
everyone, but advises the husband how to behave towards his

wife, the father how he is to bring up his children, the master how he is to control his slaves' (Letters, 94: 1). It was natural that the early Christians should also develop their own codes of this kind, as Jesus had given new insight into human relationships.

18. In instructing wives to *be subject* to their husbands, Paul started with the social order as he knew it, where the husband has the absolute authority over his household and everyone in it, including his wife. But Paul puts a different complexion on the picture when in verse 19 he interprets this authority in terms of *love*, and not tyranny. How it is their *Christian duty* is explained at greater length in Eph. 5: 22–24.

Paul had already argued that the man has authority over the woman in 1 Cor. 11: 2–16. He probably took a rather strong line there because he was nervous lest some of the claims being made by the women at Corinth should, if granted, increase the disorder in the congregation there. Whether such fears underlie our present passage, it is impossible to say. But there is every indication that Paul understood the difference that Jesus had made to the status of women (e.g. Gal. 3: 28, 'There is no such thing as Jew and Greek, slave and freeman, male and female; for you are all one person in Christ Jesus'). There are also signs that Paul saw that in marriage husband and wife are equal partners who complement each other (e.g. 1 Cor. 11: 11, 'And yet in Christ's fellowship woman is as essential to man as man to woman').

19. The theme of the husband's *love* is elaborated at greater length in Eph. 5: 25–33. The word *love*, as always in the New Testament, is coloured by the thought of the love seen in Jesus—a love that goes on giving and caring, whether it is returned or not. Such *love* cannot include what is *harsh* or 'bitter', as it 'is patient...never selfish, not quick to take offence...keeps no score of wrongs' (1 Cor. 13: 4–6).

20. Respect of *children* for their parents is to form the basis of family life. This verse may imply that children would be in the congregation when the letter was read. Such obedience

to parents is enjoined in the fifth of the Ten Commandments: 'Honour thy father and thy mother' (Exod. 20: 12; Deut. 5: 16). There is also the example of Jesus, who 'went back with them (Mary and Joseph), and continued to be under their authority' (Luke 2: 51). For these reasons such obedience *is pleasing to God and is the Christian way*. See also Eph. 6: 1–3.

21. *exasperate*, or 'embitter', is a strange term here. It probably means that parents are not to drive children to despair by demanding too much of them and by giving the impression that they can never do anything right. For further advice on the upbringing of children see on Eph. 6: 4.

22. *slaves* were part of the social and economic system of the ancient world. The slave might be employed in industry, in administration and in private households. He was technically the possession of the person whom he served, and often received good treatment. There was probably a fairly strong element of slaves in the early Church. In society slave and freeman are classes part, but in the Church the position is altered, because people are there accounted important not by reason of class but by reason of the fact that everyone is loved and wanted by Jesus (see above 3: 11). But this new status of slaves does not mean that they are to be released from their slavery, to 'get beyond themselves' and neglect their duties. We may ask: Why did not the early Church attack the existence of slavery? It was the function of the Church at that time to bring to people the good news of the Gospel. To have sought to create an economic and social upheaval would not have served this end. The spread of the Gospel would create a climate of opinion in which the social order would be reviewed and reformed. On slavery see also below, p. 179, and on the Christian attitude to it, p. 181.

earthly masters is in contrast with the heavenly Lord Jesus. Slaves are to be clear about their motives in the way that they serve their masters. They are not to put on an *outward show* of keenness with an eye to standing well with their masters, but are to act from *single-mindednes*, i.e. a pure desire to give of their best. This is what *reverence* for the will of *the Lord*, i.e. Jesus, requires.

23–24. The call to devoted service is now reinforced: slaves are to do their work as though they were doing it for Jesus himself. In this way they will be serving *a Master* who gives a far better reward for service than an earthly one, i.e. *your heritage*, which is a place in God's final kingdom (see Eph. 1: 14). *Christ is the Master whose slaves you must be*, i.e. if slaves see themselves as under the authority of Jesus, then this will affect their whole conduct.

25. *dishonesty will be requited* stresses that all Christians are accountable to Jesus (2 Cor. 5: 10, 'For we must all have our lives laid open before the tribunal of Christ'). *Dishonesty* may denote stealing. It is interesting that the same language is used of the offence of the slave Onesimus (Philem. 18, 'And if he has done you any wrong...'—the N.E.B. uses a different English expression for the same Greek word). *he has no favourites*: an important characteristic of God in the Old Testament, e.g. 2 Chron. 19: 7 ('for there is no iniquity with the Lord our God, nor respect of persons, nor taking of gifts'). It is striking how easily the early Christians applied to Jesus terms that originally applied to God.

4: 1. Similarly Christian *masters* are not 'laws to themselves' in their treatment of their slaves, even if human law would give them this right. For them there is a 'higher law', because masters, like their slaves, are under the authority of a *Master in heaven*, i.e. the Lord Jesus, and so must treat their slaves in a way worthy of him. ✱

SOME FURTHER ADVICE

Persevere in prayer, with mind awake and thankful 2 heart; and include a prayer for us, that God may give 3 us an opening for preaching, to tell the secret of Christ;

4 that indeed is why I am now in prison. Pray that I may make the secret plain, as it is my duty to do.

5   Behave wisely towards those outside your own num-
6 ber; use the present opportunity to the full. Let your conversation be always gracious, and never insipid; study how best to talk with each person you meet.

* Paul now stresses the importance of prayer, and gives advice on the correct attitude to non-Christians.

2. For the command to *persevere in prayer* see also Eph. 6: 18–20, where prayer is part of the armour supplied by God. As seen in the note on prayer at Eph. 1: 15, prayer is the means of co-operating with God. In this way we understand his purposes more fully and help forward the fulfilment of his plans for the world.

with mind awake: one of the ways in which the Christian shows that he is alert and keen for God's cause is by his attention to prayer. Jesus gave similar advice, 'Stay awake, all of you; and pray...' (Mark 14: 38). A *thankful heart* or 'thanksgiving' is often mentioned in connection with prayer (e.g. Col. 1: 2). Thanksgiving for what God has already done is an encouragement to believe that in answer to our prayers God will achieve still more.

3. Prayer is also the way in which we help other people, by laying their needs before God (2 Cor. 1: 11, 'Yes, he [God] will continue to deliver us if you will co-operate by praying for us'). So Paul here asks the Colossians to *include a prayer* for himself and his assistants. Even in prison his mind is turned towards opportunities for preaching the Gospel, and for telling *the secret of Christ*; an open secret to be told to all (see above on 1: 26–27). Paul is *now in prison* in Rome, because his preaching of the Gospel had led to the hostility of the Jews, which led in turn to his being arrested in Jerusalem (Acts 21), his appeal as a Roman citizen to the supreme court of the emperor (Acts 25: 11–12) and his subsequent journey to Rome (Acts 27–28).

4. It was Paul's *duty to do* so, as an apostle (see above on 1: 25).

5. *wisely*, in such a way as to commend the Christian Gospel. *outside your own number* is a reference to those who are not committed to the Christian faith and to membership of the Church. The early Christians felt a particular urgency in presenting the Gospel as containing the true way to God. To this end every *opportunity* should be used. For the phrase see also Eph. 5: 16.

6. *gracious*, i.e. conveying something of God's love. *never insipid*, i.e. not off-putting, but attracting people to God. Different people require different approaches. The task of preaching the Gospel is committed, we notice, to all, and not just to the Church's leaders. ✱

IMPENDING PLANS

You will hear all about my affairs from Tychicus, our 7 dear brother and trustworthy helper and fellow-servant in the Lord's work. I am sending him to you on purpose 8 to let you know all about us and to put fresh heart into you. With him comes Onesimus, our trustworthy and 9 dear brother, who is one of yourselves. They will tell you all the news here.

✱ 7. *Tychicus* had probably been known to Paul for some time. He was one of the representatives of the churches of Asia who had accompanied Paul on his journey to Jerusalem (Acts 20: 4). He has, it seems, been on a visit to Paul in Rome, and is now to convey our present letter to the church at Colossae. The suggestion was made (p. 19) that the Letter to the Ephesians may have been a manifesto specially composed by Tychicus on authority from Paul. For a similar recommendation to the one here, see Eph. 6: 21–22. In 2 Tim. 4: 12, Tychicus is said to have been sent to Ephesus, while in Tit. 3: 12

there is a proposal to send him or Artemus to Crete. The last two references perhaps suggest that Tychicus continued to be associated with Paul in his later ministry. The name Tychicus was apparently common in the area round Ephesus.

brother is a way of referring to a fellow Christian, and may also here denote that Tychicus is closely associated with Paul's work (see also above on 1: 1). *helper* is literally 'deacon', but here the reference is not to an office of deacon, but to 'one who helps forward' the work of Jesus and his church. *fellow-servant* (Greek: 'fellow-slave'). The early Christians saw themselves as the 'slaves' of their master, Jesus, as being completely under his authority, and at his disposal (see, e.g. 1 Cor. 6: 19, 'You do not belong to yourselves; you were bought at a price', i.e. like slaves).

8. *all about us*, i.e. what is happening to Paul in Rome.

9. The runaway slave *Onesimus* (a common name of slaves in the period) is the subject of the Letter to Philemon (below), written by Paul in this same period. Paul is sending him back to his master Philemon in the company of Tychicus. The description of Onesimus as *our trustworthy and dear brother* shows that he has now become a Christian, and repented of his former conduct, which may have included robbing his master (Philem. 18). Paul wishes it to be known that he has full confidence in him. ✳

FINAL GREETINGS

10 Aristarchus, Christ's captive like myself, sends his greetings; so does Mark, the cousin of Barnabas (you have had instructions about him; if he comes, make him
11 welcome), and Jesus Justus. Of the Jewish Christians, these are the only ones who work with me for the kingdom of God, and they have been a great comfort to
12 me. Greetings from Epaphras, servant of Christ, who is one of yourselves. He prays hard for you all the time,

that you may stand fast, ripe in conviction and wholly devoted to doing God's will. For I can vouch for him, 13 that he works tirelessly for you and the people at Laodicea and Hierapolis. Greetings to you from our dear friend 14 Luke, the doctor, and from Demas. Give our greetings 15 to the brothers at Laodicea, and Nympha and the congregation at her house. And when this letter is read among 16 you, see that it is also read to the congregation at Laodicea, and that you in return read the one from Laodicea. This 17 special word to Archippus: 'Attend to the duty entrusted to you in the Lord's service, and discharge it to the full.'

This greeting is in my own hand—PAUL. Remember 18 I am in prison. God's grace be with you.

✻ Paul now sends greetings from various people who are with him in Rome.

10. *Aristarchus* had probably been known to Paul since the founding of the Church at Thessalonica (Acts 17: 1–9). He is called a Thessalonian in Acts 20: 4, where he is one of the representatives of the churches who are accompanying Paul on his journey to Jerusalem. He was also with Paul on the journey to Rome (Acts 27: 2, 'In our party was Aristarchus, a Macedonian from Thessalonica'). He may have been one of the 'other prisoners' (Acts 27: 1). This may account for his being called a *captive*, i.e. he is in prison at Rome. But he is *Christ's captive*, in prison purely because of his loyalty to Jesus.

Mark is almost certainly the 'John Mark' at the house of whose mother the Christians met in the early days of the Church in Jerusalem (Acts 12: 12). He had set out with Paul and Barnabas on the important journey described in Acts 13–14, but deserted the party when they reached Perga (see Acts 13: 5 and 13). The reason is not given by Luke, but it may have been cowardice at the thought of the hazards that lay ahead. In any case the conduct of John Mark caused

Paul to mistrust him, and on a later occasion led to a rift between Paul and Barnabas, who 'wanted to take John Mark with them' (Acts 15: 37–39). Mark has by now, it seems, proved himself and is restored to Paul's confidence. Later in 2 Tim. 4: 11 he is called a 'useful assistant', and is by tradition the writer of our second Gospel. The earlier dispute was probably heightened because he was, as here described, the *cousin of Barnabas*.

Barnabas was obviously an important figure in the early days of the Church, and was one of the early converts to Christianity (Acts 4: 36-37). He was a sponsor and champion of Paul in the latter's early career as an apostle (Acts 9: 27). He also paved the way for Paul's work in the Church at Antioch (Acts 11: 22–26), and is associated with him on the journey to Jerusalem undertaken 'for the relief of their fellow-Christians in Judaea' (Acts 11: 29–30). Paul and he were commissioned by the Church at Antioch to undertake the important journey (Acts 13–14) which led to the establishment of churches in Asia Minor. In the problems about gentile Christians, Paul tells us that 'even Barnabas...played false' (Gal. 2: 13), but Barnabas stands firmly with Paul at the Council of Jerusalem (Acts 15). It was after this that the dispute arose over John Mark. Amicable relations appear to have been restored, as later he mentions himself in conjunction with Barnabas (1 Cor. 9: 6). *Jesus Justus*—mentioned only here. *Jesus* was a common Jewish name. *Justus* was his Greek name which he had adopted probably because he belonged to a Greek city.

11. This suggests that Paul was still viewed with some suspicion by the Jewish Christian section of the Church. Perhaps they mistrusted one who had persecuted the Church when it consisted of Jewish Christians like themselves. They may also have resented what they thought to be Paul's belittlement of the Jewish law. He may have had an eye on this accusation when in his letter to the Church at Rome he says, 'What follows? Is the law identical with sin? Of course

not' (Rom. 7: 7). On *the kingdom of God* see above 1: 13 and Eph. 5: 5.

12. For *Epaphras* see above on 1: 7. *ripe in conviction*, i.e. all-out committal to the Christian faith. Another translation could be 'mature and complete', i.e. in understanding and living out the Gospel.

13. *Laodicea* has already been mentioned in 2: 1; *Hierapolis* was a city in the same area. For both see also, p. 112 and map p. ix.

14. *Luke* is also mentioned in the concluding greeting of the letter to Philemon (23–24), where he is called one of Paul's 'fellow-workers'. 2 Tim. 4: 11 ('I have no one with me but Luke') may suggest that he was Paul's only companion during a later imprisonment at Rome. He is sometimes thought to be the same person as Lucius of Cyrene, who is mentioned among the prophets and teachers of the Church at Antioch (Acts 13: 1). If this is so, Paul may have first met him at Antioch. By tradition he is the author of the Gospel of Luke and the Acts of the Apostles, two volumes of a single work. In certain passages of the Acts the person changes from 'they' to 'we' (e.g. 16: 10, 'after he had seen this vision we at once set about getting a passage to Macedonia'). This implies that the author is present with Paul on these occasions, which include his journey to and arrival in Rome (27: 1 — 28: 16). The last passage fits in very well with what our present passage tells us: that Luke is with Paul during his imprisonment at Rome. Luke *the doctor* may have been using his medical skill in caring for Paul's health during his imprisonment. *Demas* is mentioned in the greeting at the end of Philemon (23–24). From 2 Tim. 4: 10 it seems that later he deserted Paul, 'because his heart was set on this world'.

15. *brothers* means 'fellow Christians'. *Nympha*, mentioned only here. In the Greek the word could be a masculine or feminine name, depending on whether *her* or *his* is thought to be the right reading later in the sentence. The Christian congregations had no special buildings at this time, but met in

private houses (see also e.g. Rom. 16: 3–5, 'Give my greetings to Prisca and Aquila...Greet also the congregation at their house'). Whether Nympha lived at Laodicea is uncertain.

16. This is important evidence (*a*) that Paul's letters were meant to be read to the whole congregation, probably during its Sunday act of worship (see also 1 Thess. 5: 27), and (*b*) that they were sometimes passed from church to church. *the one from Laodicea* means the letter that Paul had sent to that congregation (probably not our Letter to the Ephesians, as sometimes suggested).

17. For *Archippus* (a common name in this period) see Philem. 2, where he is described as a 'comrade-in-arms' of Paul and Timothy. He seems to have had a post of special leadership in the Colossian church. Perhaps *the duty entrusted to you* is that of defending the Gospel against the propaganda that was being aimed at the Colossian church. For another possibility see below, p. 174.

18. In accordance with the custom of the times Paul would normally dictate his letter or commission it to be written and add the final section in his own handwriting. The *greeting* might refer to 4: 10–18, but more probably means simply 4: 18. Paul draws attention to the change in the handwriting for the benefit of those who would hear the letter read and would not see it for themselves. *Remember* is commonly taken as a reference to prayer; it might, however, mean that under the conditions of his imprisonment he has been forced to leave a lot of the composition of the letter to his secretary. Reference to *God's grace* is usual in the conclusion of Paul's letters: see on Eph. 6: 23–24. The conclusion in letters of Paul's time was usually 'fare you well'—an expression of good wishes. As, however, with the opening greeting, so here, Paul introduces a term that will strike home to the Christian.

✻   ✻   ✻   ✻   ✻   ✻   ✻   ✻   ✻   ✻   ✻   ✻   ✻

(1) *Compromise*

The big challenge and temptation being held out to the Colossian Christians was to compromise with the other religions of the day and, in accordance with the thought of the times, to combine faith in Jesus Christ with belief in other powers. Paul's answer was in terms of 'no compromise'. A willingness to compromise is often thought to be a virtue today, and the attitude of Paul might seem rigid and harsh. The letter calls us to think more seriously about the word 'compromise'.

Compromise is often an essential to the making of agreements. Each side may withdraw certain demands or accept modifications of its position in order to come to terms and a working arrangement. A demand may be withdrawn in response to a concession by the other side. Compromise or a willingness to 'give and take' must be a prominent feature of all human relationships at all levels. Absence of this would be taking up the attitude that one's own demands and ways should be accepted unquestioningly by others—an attitude that could only arise from a sense of pride and lack of respect for other people. A lack of the spirit of compromise would make all discussion unprofitable and agreement between people impossible.

But there are fields where a 'no compromise' attitude is justifiable. In the first place, it is true of moral conviction. To hold a certain moral standard may result and must result in a refusal to compromise and accept or imitate the actions and attitudes of people who do not accept that standard. Here, to compromise would be to part with one's integrity, and go against conscience and conviction. Such a 'no compromise' attitude is not being rigid and stiff, but the result of the recognition that there are values in life which cannot be ignored.

The other field where the same applies is that of truth. To

have the conviction that *A* is correct and *B* is not in accordance with fact means that one has a duty to act on *A*. For the scientist who has a 'hunch' that *A* is a working hypothesis and *B* is a hypothesis that will lead nowhere, there can be no compromise; he has to follow the first. Paul's teaching that there can be no accommodation with the 'syncretism' at Colossae is a 'no compromise' decision of this kind. On the basis of the evidence available to him Paul is convinced that only the 'Jesus Christ hypothesis' holds the key to being right with God; to give way on this issue and to compromise would be wrong and dishonest. In other words, toleration—the state of affairs where all have the opportunity of expressing their own views—is a good thing and an important element in modern democracy. But it is not the equivalent of giving up one's own convictions or resigning the duty of passing them on to others.

(2) *The uniqueness of Jesus Christ*

The opinion is sometimes expressed that all religions are in reality the same and that all of them alike have something equally valuable to offer; there is not much to choose between them. A similar view was held in the contemporary world of Paul, where it was thought natural to combine different religions. Such a view needs further analysis.

All religions are the same in the sense that they are all important witness and evidence of man's feeling for and search for what has been called 'the wholly other', the divine power behind the universe. They have, too, the common factor that they all offer in various ways a solution and answer to this human quest. In varying degrees they all give human beings help and hope in the living of their lives and in facing death.

But this does not rule out the fact that one religion may be more advanced than another in claiming to bring a deeper understanding of God and a closer union with him, and to shed more light on the meaning of human life.

The claim of Christianity to such a special position can be briefly stated as follows:

(*a*) God makes special provision in and through the Jewish nation for revealing himself to the whole world. The Old Testament contains the account of how the Jews came to believe in the One God, the creator and sustainer of the whole universe, who is righteous and demands righteousness, and holds out the hope that he will make himself even better known in the future.

(*b*) In Jesus Christ that hope is fulfilled; he is the climax of Jewish history in the sense that he brings that deeper revelation of God to which the Jews looked forward.

(*c*) In Jesus Christ, a historical person, God entered directly into the life of this planet and confronted us in a person of flesh and blood, who (to use the description of 1 John 1: 1) was 'heard', 'seen', 'looked upon' and 'felt'. We note Col. 1: 19 with its tremendous claim: 'For in him the complete being of God, by God's own choice, came to dwell.' The unique thing about the Christian religion is the belief that 'the Word became flesh; he came to dwell among us...' (John 1: 14); the being and nature of God have been revealed in a human life and death. The Christian claim is that God has come to closer quarters with his creation and has revealed his true nature of love more clearly in Jesus Christ than in any other religion.

(*d*) In the 'come-back' of Jesus at his Resurrection, God has given a unique demonstration that his cause and purposes will be achieved.

The Letter to the Colossians with its dogmatic assertion of the uniqueness of Jesus Christ challenges the assumption that all religions are the same, with something equally valuable to offer. Rather it claims that the Christian faith gives *the* answer for which all religions are looking.

(3) *Human fears and anxieties*

The challenge to the Colossian Church was very much occupied with playing on fear of the influence that the planetary powers could have on human destiny. Fear of and a desire to be right with his environment has always been a feature of man's life. Groping after security is one of the human quests. The natural world has held its terrors, but scientific discovery and the harnessing of the forces of nature have taken a lot of the sting out of these. Yet people's interest in horoscopes, published in the newspapers, and in 'reading the stars' suggests that the unhealthy superstitions of Paul's day are not wholly ended. Such predictions, especially if they concern misfortune, can have a bad effect on people's minds. But the 'cosmic powers' and 'authorities' of which Paul speaks really stand for the anxieties of different kinds that cloud people's existence in every age, though maybe only at the subconscious level. Perhaps a list of modern anxieties might run as follows:

the feeling of guilt at wrong done to someone;
the feeling of loneliness—that 'nobody cares';
the sense of failure—that one is not keeping up with success and is not making the grade;
the sense of the futility of life, perhaps that arising from the danger of men using science to destroy themselves;
the sense of being at loggerheads with life.

Whether always realized or not, the need for security is deep in everyone, and an important element in this need is the desire to 'feel wanted'. Paul claims in the letter to the Colossians that this kind of security is found in reconciliation with God, who has gone out of his way to show that he cares for us (1: 22, 'But now by Christ's death in his body of flesh and blood God has reconciled you to himself'). He has assured us of his forgiveness (1: 13, 'He...brought us away into the kingdom of his dear Son, in whom our release is secured and our sins forgiven') and holds out the hope of life with him here and now and in the future (1: 27, 'The secret is this: Christ in you, the hope of a glory to come'). At the basis of this security is the fact that God has placed himself alongside us in the historical Jesus Christ, and Jesus' own life of obedience to and confidence in God is the very negation of human fears (2: 15). Paul's remedy, therefore, for anxiety and fear is the conviction that he expresses in his letter to the Romans 8: 38: 'For I am convinced that there is nothing in death or life...nothing in all creation that can separate us from the love of God in Christ Jesus our Lord'. Colossians throws out the challenge that Christianity has something to say to human fears and anxieties.

(4) *Christianity and 'other-worldliness'*

The Christian Church has often been accused of supporting the attitude that Christians should not be over-concerned about this world. Such a passage as Col. 3: 1–2 ('Then aspire to the realm above, where Christ is, seated at the right hand of God, and let your thoughts dwell on that higher realm, not on this earthly life') might wrongly (as already seen, p. 150) be thought to give grounds for such an accusation. The question is therefore to be raised: In what sense is Christianity 'other-worldly'?

(*a*) The Christian life is 'other-worldly' in the sense that its terms of reference are not to be found purely and simply in the visible world, and that it brings in a category other than the observable in order to explain human life. From the Christian viewpoint, human beings are not merely further samples and specimens of biological life, but are personal beings created to worship a personal God of love, who, though involved in his world, also transcends it. *Any* theory that gives human life a *purpose* and introduces values of human conduct and does not believe the world to be self-explanatory must be 'other-worldly' in this sense.

(*b*) The Christian faith is also 'other-worldly' in that it teaches that the relationship of the Christian with Jesus Christ is not severed by physical death, and encourages the hope of a fuller and closer union with him.

(c) The Christian faith is 'other-worldly', too, because it holds out the hope, however dimly discerned, that God will bring into being an order of things where his purposes are complete and he will be 'all in all'.

(d) But this 'other-worldliness' does not mean a neglect of the present world, and of life on this planet as it is at the moment. The 'other-worldly' Christian 'philosophy of life' means that Christians see present life as having a very definite purpose. There is the Christian attitude of mind to contemporary problems, towards people and things; the belief that at the heart of the universe there is a God of love, with the corollary that this love must inform human relationships here and now and our use of 'the things' with which the universe provides us. If people are loved by God, then they are never to be used as 'mere tools', but as real and valued human beings.

Further, in view of God's revelation of himself in 'flesh and blood', Christianity is the most materialistic of religions. In Christian thought, then, the distinction between sacred and secular does not exist, as the whole of the material world is shot through with opportunities to be used for God's service.

✳ ✳ ✳ ✳ ✳ ✳ ✳ ✳ ✳ ✳ ✳ ✳ ✳

THE LETTER OF PAUL TO

PHILEMON

✳　✳　✳　✳　✳　✳　✳　✳　✳　✳　✳　✳　✳

A PERSONAL LETTER OF PAUL

The letter to Philemon is found among the earliest collections of Paul's letters, and there is no valid reason for doubting that it is a genuine letter of Paul. It differs from the other letters of Paul in that this letter resembles more a personal note about a personal matter. The usual explanation is that the letter is intended particularly for Philemon (verse 1). He is considered to be the master of the slave Onesimus, who has run away and somehow joined Paul. In the main body of the letter (verses 4–24), 'you' must refer to one person, as it is singular in the Greek; it is normally thought that Philemon is that person. An alternative suggestion has, however, been made: 'the congregation at your house' (verse 2), which is usually taken to refer to the house of Philemon, is on this view thought to refer to that of Archippus, who has been mentioned immediately before. It follows that in verse 4 'you', which in the Greek is singular, means Archippus ('I thank my God always when I mention you in my prayers'). In that case, Archippus, 'our comrade-in-arms' (verse 2), would be the master of the slave Onesimus, and the main body of the letter is addressed to him. On this theory, Archippus was not known to Paul, and so Philemon, Apphia and the church in the house of Archippus are included in the opening address in the hope that they will support his appeal. Philemon and Apphia, it is surmised, lived at Laodicea, and are mentioned first because Tychicus (see below, p. 177) and Onesimus on their way to Colossae would call first at Laodicea (see map, p. ix) and would leave the letter with them. Philemon would then bring or send it to Archippus at Colossae, and it would also receive the attention of the Christian congregation that met at his house. This congregation is thought to be identical with 'God's people at Colossae', to whom the Letter to the Colossians is written. The Letter to Philemon is then regarded as that 'from Laodicea', which is mentioned in Col. 4: 16 just before Paul sends a special message to Archippus (Col. 4: 17, 'This special word to Archippus: "Attend to the duty entrusted to you in the Lord's service, and discharge it to the full"'). On this view, the 'duty entrusted' to Archippus is that of allowing Onesimus to return to Paul to help him in his work.

This theory, while it has its attractions, is also very speculative; and here the more normal view is accepted, that Philemon is the main recipient of the letter, which is also to be brought to the attention of Apphia and Archippus and the Christians that met at Philemon's house. It is not, therefore, confidential.

The Letter to Philemon has sometimes suffered from comparison with the other letters of Paul. Compared with the major issues of Christian teaching that Paul deals with, e.g. in Romans and Ephesians, its theme may seem to be trivial. But, as we shall see, Paul is here applying the lofty truths of the Christian to the 'daily round' and the ordinary situations of life.

WHERE WAS PHILEMON WRITTEN?

We are not told in the letter of the place from which Paul is writing. All we know of his situation is that he is in prison. He speaks of himself as the 'prisoner' of Jesus (verses 1 and 9) and tells us that he has become the 'father' of the slave Onesimus 'in this prison' (verse 10). Similarly Paul says that he longs to keep Onesimus with him, 'here in prison for the Gospel' (verse 13). The description of Epaphras as 'Christ's captive like myself' may imply the same. There is a strong tradition that Philemon was written from Rome during the imprisonment of Paul described in Acts 28: 16, 'When we entered Rome Paul was allowed to lodge by himself with a soldier in charge of him'. This imprisonment lasted at least two years (Acts 28: 30, 'He stayed there two full years at his own expense'). An introduction to Colossians about A.D. 180 suggests Ephesus as the place of writing, but this is exceptional.

In more recent times several arguments have been brought forward against the firm tradition that Philemon was written at Rome, and they may be briefly mentioned here.

(i) The runaway slave, Onesimus, has made good his escape from his master Philemon and has come into contact with Paul (verse 13, 'I should have liked to keep him with me'). But it is thought more reasonable to suppose that Onesimus made his escape to somewhere like Caesarea or Ephesus (places much nearer to Colossae, see map, p. ix). It is easier to understand that Onesimus joined Paul at one of these places than to imagine that he made the long journey to Rome. If such a view is plausible, then we should have to say that Philemon was written during an imprisonment at Caesarea or Ephesus. There is evidence for Paul having been imprisoned at Caesarea (Acts 23: 33–35, 'The cavalry entered Caesarea, delivered the letter to the Governor, and handed Paul over to him...He then ordered him to be held in custody at his headquarters in Herod's palace'). The evidence for an imprisonment at Ephesus is very weak, and has no support in the New Testament (see above, p. 115).

It may therefore seem plausible to think that Philemon (and the same would apply to Colossians) was written from Caesarea, the capital and administrative centre of the Roman province of Judaea. But on the other hand it is easy to underestimate the facilities for travel in the ancient world. Philem. 18 implies that Onesimus had robbed his master of money, and he may well have used some of this to book himself a passage for Rome! Here he may have thought that he could remain hidden and disappear much more satisfactorily than in Asia Minor.

(ii) In Philem. 22 Paul expresses the hope of paying an early visit to Colossae: 'have a room ready for me, for I hope that, in answer to your prayers, God will grant me to you'. This hope is thought to be more natural if he is in prison, e.g. in Caesarea, than if he is in Rome where his attention was concentrated on a visit to Spain in the event of his liberation from imprisonment.

It is true that Paul in his letter to the Romans looks forward to his coming visit to Spain, and says: 'So when I have finished this business and delivered the proceeds under my own seal, I shall set out for Spain by way of your city' (15: 28). But when Paul expresses this intention, he does not know that he will go to Rome as a prisoner, and in Rome he may well have changed his plans about what he would do when he was freed. He may well have thought that a visit to Asia Minor should have priority over a visit to Spain. The question of the distance from Colossae would not have daunted him, any more than the distance from Spain.

None of the arguments above is conclusive against the firm tradition that Philemon was written from Rome. This still remains the best possibility, and here it is accepted that Philemon belongs to the imprisonment in Rome, the beginning of which is described in Acts 28: 16.

WHEN WAS PHILEMON WRITTEN?

It is impossible to determine the exact date when the letter was written, but it obviously belongs to the same period as Colossians; for there are close connections between the two letters. In the first place, the slave Onesimus is being sent back to his master Philemon. Paul speaks of this in Philem. 12, 'I am sending him back to you'. This links up with Col. 4: 9, 'With him [Tychicus] comes Onesimus, our trustworthy and dear brother'. Again, there are a number of people who are with Paul and send greetings at the end of the letter to the Colossians. Among these are Epaphras, Mark, Aristarchus,

Demas and Luke. They are mentioned also in the greetings at the end of Philemon (verses 23–24). Another connection between the letters is the mention of Archippus (Philem. 2), for whom Paul also has a special word in Col. 4: 17. The two letters date, therefore, to about the same time during Paul's imprisonment at Rome in the period A.D. 59 onwards. Its destination was obviously Colossae, and it was probably conveyed there by Tychicus, 'our dear brother and trustworthy helper and fellow-servant in the Lord's work' (Col. 4: 7), who was almost certainly entrusted with the delivery of Colossians. For Tychicus and his connection with Paul see above, p. 18.

PHILEMON, 'OUR DEAR FRIEND AND FELLOW-WORKER'—WHO WAS HE?

Philemon was clearly an inhabitant of Colossae who had been brought to Christianity by Paul himself (Philem. 19), probably during Paul's ministry at Ephesus. Since then he had been active in the service of Jesus Christ (Philem. 5), by giving support to his fellow Christians and probably by making his home the meeting-place of Christians at Colossae (Philem. 12). There are later traditions that he became bishop of Colossae or of Gaza, and died the death of a martyr at Colossae during the persecution of Christians in the time of the Emperor Nero (A.D. 64). Apphia is coupled with Philemon in the opening greeting. She is probably his wife, and, as the mistress of the household, was very much concerned with what had happened to Onesimus.

WHO WAS ONESIMUS?

The name, which means 'useful', was commonly held by slaves, or by freedmen, i.e. those who had been slaves but had been given their freedom. Onesimus had been a slave in the household of Philemon (Philem. 15–16 '...that you might have him back for good, no longer as a slave, but as more than a slave'). Slaves of that area had a notoriously bad reputation. Onesimus had lived up to it. He had run away, robbing his master in the process (verse 18, 'And if he has done you any wrong or is in your debt...'). He had taken refuge in Rome, no doubt thinking that there he could easily disappear and never be hunted down.

Somehow he came into contact with Paul, who was a prisoner in Rome and who was probably known to him at least by reputation. Whether in Rome Onesimus met Paul by accident or design, we do not know. Under Paul's guidance he became a Christian (verse 10, 'my child, whose father I have become in this prison'), and a strong attachment arose between the two (verses 12–13). Paul would have liked to keep Onesimus with him at Rome. But he knew that it was the slave's duty to face the situation by returning to his master and making up for what he had done wrong (verses 12 and 15). Paul offers his own security for any money owed by Onesimus (verse 18).

The later history of Onesimus is not known very clearly. The theory has been put forward that it was he who had the idea of collecting Paul's letters or even that he wrote Ephesians as an introduction to them (see above, p. 16). But this is speculation. Bishop Ignatius of Antioch, writing to the church at Ephesus in the period A.D. 98–117, speaks of 'Onesimus, a man of indescribable love and your bishop' (Ephesians 1: 3). But it is not at all certain that this bishop of Ephesus and our Onesimus are one and the same, especially as the name is a common one. The same uncertainty attaches to the tradition that he died the death of a martyr.

PAUL'S APPROACH TO THE PROBLEM

Paul's letter to Philemon is really one of recommendation, and can be paralleled by other letters that have survived from this period and are on a similar subject. The younger Pliny, for example, who was born A.D. 61, and who later was governor of Bithynia (A.D. 111–113), wrote a letter on behalf of an offending freedman, which begins as follows:

'C. Plinius to his friend Sabinianus greeting. Your freedman, with whom you said you were angry, came to me, flung himself at my feet, and clung there as if they were yours. He was profuse in his tears and his entreaties; there was much too that he left unsaid. But in a word he convinced me of his change of heart. I have real confidence that he is a changed character, because he is conscious that he has done wrong. You will be angry, I realize, and rightly angry, as I also realize; but clemency is most to be praised when the reason for anger is of the most legitimate kind. You have loved the man, and I hope that you will love him...' (*Letters*, 9, 21).

It is interesting to note that Paul is writing on behalf of someone who in the eyes of the law had no rights. The slave was strictly the property of his master and at his mercy. The institution of slavery was part of the social and economic system of the ancient world. The slave might be employed in industry, in administration and in private households. But, however great the responsibility he was given, he was none the less technically a piece of property. This could easily lead to his being regarded as a different kind of human being from freemen. Against this degrading view of the slave, thinking people in Paul's day were already beginning to raise a voice of protest. For example, the Roman politician and author Seneca, who was a contemporary of Paul, asserts that a slave can confer a benefit on his master as one man to another. The Stoics (see above, p. 20) recognized the slave as a member of the city of gods and men. At the end of the first century A.D. Dio Chrysostom, the Greek author, points out that the distinction between slave and freeman has no basis in nature. Paul and the early Christians could make a telling contribution to this discussion. In the first place, a slave was noble and valuable, because he was one of the human race for whom Jesus died (e.g. 2 Cor. 5: 14, 'For the love of Christ leaves us no choice, when once we have reached the conclusion that one man died for all and therefore all mankind has died'). There is the *one* Lord Jesus claiming the allegiance of both master and slave. In the second place, the word 'slave' is no longer a term of degradation and abuse, because Christians are proud to be called 'slaves' of Jesus. Paul himself, a freeman and a Roman citizen, describes himself as a slave of Jesus (Rom. 1: 1, 'From Paul, servant [literally 'slave'] of Christ Jesus'). Therefore, all through the letter to Philemon Paul's approach is coloured by the thought that 'there is no such thing as Jew and Greek, slave and freeman, male and female; for you are all one person in Christ Jesus' (Gal. 3: 28).

First, Paul underlines that the starting-point in this problem, as in all others, is the bond between Philemon and himself created by their joint service of Jesus (verse 6, 'My prayer is that your fellowship with us in our common faith may deepen the understanding of all the blessings that our union with Christ brings us'). That bond is one of love, and, between people who love, the correct approach is for one to *appeal* to the other. Therefore Paul will not use his authority as an apostle to tell Philemon what to do (verses 8–10). He will not force the issue by detaining Onesimus with him in Rome, and so denying to Philemon his right of dealing with the matter (verses 13–14, 'I should have liked to keep him with me...But I would rather do nothing without your consent'). This would have been a betrayal of trust. But in commending Onesimus to the generosity of Philemon, Paul points out that it cannot be a case of 'master–slave' relationship. For Onesimus is now a fellow Christian and also dear to Paul (verse 16, '...no longer as a slave, but as more than a slave—as a dear brother, very dear indeed to me and how much dearer to you, both as man and as Christian'). There is also a warm appeal to the fact that Philemon in his loving treatment of Onesimus will be doing a service to Paul, a fellow Christian, to whom Philemon owes his own belief in Jesus Christ (verses 17–20).

It is to be noticed that Paul does not ask Philemon to give Onesimus his freedom. Paul's interest centres on his concern that love should be the determining factor between the master and the slave. There is only one passage in his letters where Paul has been thought to recommend slaves to accept their freedom if it is offered to them. This is 1 Cor. 7: 21, where the N.E.B. translates: 'Were you a slave when you were called? Do not let that trouble you; but if a chance of liberty should come, take it.' But the whole context and Greek text are rather in favour of the alternative translation mentioned in the N.E.B. footnote: 'but even if a chance of liberty should come, choose rather to make good use of your servitude.' The question is therefore raised: Why did not the early Church attack the existence of slavery? It would be easy to exaggerate the influence on this question of the belief that the present world-order was coming to an end, e.g. 1 Cor. 7: 31, 'For the whole frame of this world is passing away'. The early Church saw its task as that of bringing to people the good news of the Gospel. To have sought to create an economic and social upheaval would not have served this end. The spread of the Gospel, with its impact on human relationships, would create a climate of opinion in which the social order would be reviewed and reformed.

✳   ✳   ✳   ✳   ✳   ✳   ✳   ✳   ✳   ✳   ✳   ✳   ✳

A Runaway Slave

OPENING GREETING

FROM PAUL, a prisoner of Christ Jesus, and our colleague Timothy, to Philemon our dear friend and
2 fellow-worker, and Apphia our sister, and Archippus our comrade-in-arms, and the congregation at your house.

3 Grace to you and peace from God our Father and the Lord Jesus Christ.

✻ The opening follows the pattern of the other letters of Paul. Letters of the time began: 'So-and-so to so-and-so greeting'. Paul follows this general outline, but substitutes the important Christian words *grace* and *peace* for the normal word 'greeting'. In the Greek 'greeting' and *grace* are very similar to each other. 'Peace be with you' was a common Jewish greeting.

1. Paul is a *prisoner* in Rome (see above p. 174) awaiting the hearing of his case before the emperor's supreme court. But he will not describe himself as the emperor's prisoner, but as the *prisoner of Christ Jesus*. In this way Paul expresses the fact that (*a*) his imprisonment has been the result of his loyalty to Jesus in preaching the Gospel; and (*b*) his whole life has been captured by Jesus and by the need to serve him (Phil. 3: 12, 'Christ once took hold of me').

Paul usually mentions his status of apostle at this point (e.g. 1 Cor. 1: 1) to show that he has the authority of Jesus for writing. Here he omits such a reference because he does not wish to appeal to his authority in his plea on behalf of Onesimus (verses 8–10). The word *prisoner* will touch the heart of Philemon.

Timothy had been a loyal and trusted assistant of Paul for

some years past (see above, p. 128). In other letters, as here,
he is also closely associated with Paul in the opening greeting
(e.g. Col. 1: 1). *colleague* (Greek: 'brother') usually describes
a 'fellow Christian'. Here it may also denote the close
connection between himself and Paul in their work.

Philemon (see above, p. 177) was a *fellow-worker* i.e. in
furthering the cause of Jesus. *Apphia* was probably the wife
of Philemon, and as a fellow Christian is described as *our
sister*. *Archippus* may have been the son of *Philemon* and
Apphia. He seems to have had a post of special responsibility
in the Church at Colossae (Col. 4: 17). The Christian is
sometimes pictured as a warrior fighting the cause of Jesus,
and therefore *Archippus* can be described as *comrade-in-arms*
or 'fellow-soldier'. The Christian congregations had no
special buildings for their meetings; they used private houses.
your almost certainly refers to Philemon.

congregation or 'church' had described the Jews as a people
in a special relationship to God. It is now used of those who
are reconciled to God through the work of Jesus.

3. This is almost a prayer that those addressed may share
the full benefits of God's *grace*, i.e. his love and favour
revealed in Jesus, and of his *peace*, i.e. his offer of friendship
and reconciliation. We notice the close connection between
God and *Jesus*. It is through Jesus' life and work that we are
put in touch with God and know his love. Therefore God
can be called *our Father*. Jesus taught his followers to address
God as 'Our Father' (Matt. 6: 9; and see also Gal. 4: 6, 'To
prove that you are sons, God has sent into our hearts the
Spirit of his Son, crying "Abba! Father!"'). *Jesus* is the human
name. *Christ* (literally 'the Anointed One') was originally a
title, denoting Jesus as the expected King of the Jews. It then
became part of his name. *Lord* is a title of the risen and
exalted Jesus. It describes his divinity and the allegiance that
he expects from his followers, and depicts him as the one
in whom God reclaims lordship over his world. For *Lord
Jesus Christ* see further above, p. 30. This close connection

between God and Jesus led to rethinking about the nature of God, and to the formulation of the doctrine of the Trinity (see above, p. 64). ✳

THANKSGIVING

4 I thank my God always when I mention you in my
5 prayers, for I hear of your love and faith towards the
6 Lord Jesus and towards all God's people. My prayer is that your fellowship with us in our common faith may deepen the understanding of all the blessings that our
7 union with Christ brings us. For I am delighted and encouraged by your love: through you, my brother, God's people have been much refreshed.

✳ Paul often, as here, begins on a note of thanksgiving, and assures those addressed of his prayers for them (see also Col. 1: 3). For the importance of prayer for Jesus and the early Church see above, p. 40.

4–5. Paul firmly believes that *prayers* to God for other people are one of the ways in which they are helped to be loyal to him and are given his strength. *You* refers back to Philemon; the Greek makes it clear that one person is meant. But the laying of Philemon's needs before God cannot but lead to an expression of thanksgiving or gratitude to God. For Paul receives news of Philemon's *love and faith towards the Lord Jesus and towards all God's people*. Paul means that Philemon's *love and faith towards the Lord Jesus*, i.e. his full committal and obedience to Jesus and his message have a further result. They lead to a deep love for other human beings and especially *God's people*, one's fellow Christians, with whom one is in close contact. *God's people* is literally 'those set apart', i.e. those who are dedicated and devoted to God's cause (see also above on Eph. 1: 1).

6. The last part of the verse might be translated: 'the

understanding of all the blessings that are among us, to the
honour of Christ', i.e. the credit for these blessings goes
wholly to him. In any case, the point of Paul's prayer is that
Philemon's *faith*, or acceptance of Jesus as Lord, may be
accompanied by ever-growing *understanding* or appreciation
of the blessings that Jesus Christ has brought. These blessings
include, for example, a deeper knowledge of God's love.

7. Such *understanding* is already shown in a practical
way by Philemon's love. *refreshed* probably includes not only
monetary help, but all kinds of assistance, e.g. encouragement of fellow Christians and providing of facilities for
Christians to meet. *brother*: an affectionate term for a fellow
Christian. ✳

PAUL'S APPROACH TO PHILEMON

Accordingly, although in Christ I might make bold to 8
point out your duty, yet, because of that same love, I 9
would rather appeal to you. Yes, I, Paul, ambassador as
I am of Christ Jesus—and now his prisoner—appeal to 10
you about my child, whose father I have become in this
prison.

✳ Paul will not use his authority to tell Philemon how to
treat Onesimus. He prefers to commend Onesimus to
Philemon's generous love, already mentioned.

8–10. *in Christ*, i.e. through or by virtue of his position
as an apostle in the Church, Paul might have laid down a
ready-made solution as to where Philemon's *duty* lay. But
Paul knows that appeal to authority is really out of place
in a fellowship where *love* is the main force at work. He
therefore prefers to rely on an appeal to the generous love
of Philemon, and leaves him to make his decision.

ambassador describes Paul as the representative of Jesus with
powers to speak for him. *prisoners*—an unusual condition

for an envoy, who would have diplomatic immunity (see also Eph. 6: 19). Paul has the status of ambassador, and, as we might say, his prestige is even more enhanced by the fact that he is in prison for his beliefs. Yet he prefers not to rely on position and status, but to *appeal* to Philemon as one Christian to another.

But it is equally possible to translate the passage: 'I, Paul, the old man as I am, and now also the prisoner of Jesus Christ'. In that case the meaning is that Paul will not exercise any influence that his advancing years and seniority in age might give him.

my child: the slave Onesimus is now referred to for the first time. *child* is an affectionate term for Christians, used by those who have special care and responsibility for other Christians, e.g. 3 John 4, 'Nothing gives me greater joy than to hear that my children are living by the truth'.

Paul had become the *father* of Onesimus in the sense that he had brought the latter to belief in Jesus and membership of the Church. In a similar way Paul says of the Corinthians, 'You may have ten thousand tutors in Christ, but you have only one father. For in Christ Jesus you are my offspring, and mine alone, through the preaching of the Gospel' (1 Cor. 4: 15). *in this prison* does not necessarily mean that Onesimus is imprisoned too. All it need mean is that he had visited Paul in prison. Both at Caesarea and at Rome Paul was allowed visitors (Acts 24: 23; 28: 30). ✳

PAUL'S ACTION ABOUT ONESIMUS

11 I mean Onesimus, once so little use to you, but now
12 useful indeed, both to you and to me. I am sending him
back to you, and in doing so I am sending a part of
13 myself. I should have liked to keep him with me, to look
after me as you would wish, here in prison for the Gospel.
14 But I would rather do nothing without your consent, so

that your kindness may be a matter not of compulsion,
but of your own free will. For perhaps this is why you 15
lost him for a time, that you might have him back for
good, no longer as a slave, but as more than a slave—as 16
a dear brother, very dear indeed to me and how much
dearer to you, both as man and as Christian.

✻ Paul is sending back Onesimus to Philemon.

11. There is a play here on the name, Onesimus, which
means 'useful'. He had been an unreliable slave, and in that
sense *little use*. But he was now *useful*, because he had shown
himself responsible in looking after Paul in prison, and
because he was now a Christian. Who knew what possi-
bilities there might be for his serving Jesus Christ?

12. *a part of myself* (Greek: 'my heart' or 'my love')
shows the close attachment that has sprung up between
Onesimus and Paul.

13–14. Paul could have detained Onesimus at Rome on the
grounds that he was looking after the welfare of the apostle
and that this would be the wish of Philemon. But this action
would have meant imposing a solution of the problem on
Philemon, forcing his hand and interfering with something
that was another's responsibility. The only fair way was for
Onesimus to return to Philemon, who by law owned his
slave, and for Philemon to make a decision about him,
according to his Christian lights.

15–16. *lost him*, i.e. when Onesimus ran away from his
post in Philemon's household. As the slave is now a fellow
Christian (*a dear brother*), the relationship cannot be that of
master and slave, but must be that of Christian and Christian;
for 'there is no question here of...freeman, slave; but Christ
is all, and is in all' (Col. 3: 11). Because of this permanent
bond between the two, Philemon has Onesimus *back for
good*. ✻

PAUL'S APPEAL

17 If, then, you count me partner in the faith, welcome him
18 as you would welcome me. And if he has done you any
wrong or is in your debt, put that down to my account.
19 Here is my signature, PAUL; I undertake to repay—
not to mention that you owe your very self to me as
20 well. Now brother, as a Christian, be generous with me,
and relieve my anxiety; we are both in Christ!
21   I write to you confident that you will meet my wishes;
22 I know that you will in fact do better than I ask. And
one thing more: have a room ready for me, for I hope
that, in answer to your prayers, God will grant me to you.

✻ Paul offers to make reparation for any loss (probably
financial) that Philemon had suffered when Onesimus ran
away.

17. Paul appeals to the fact that he and Philemon are
partners, sharing a common belief in Jesus Christ and a
desire to serve him.

18. The *wrong* and the *debt* might be due to the fact that
Onesimus had stolen money or goods from Philemon when
he ran away. Paul speaks like a merchant who wants something debited to his account.

19. Paul (rather light-heartedly perhaps) adds his signature
giving authority for the 'debit'. Probably up to this point
Paul has dictated the letter to his secretary; now, according
to his custom and the custom of the time, he writes the
concluding section in his own hand (see above, p. 6 and
Col. 4: 18). Again, perhaps rather humorously, Paul points
out that to offset the present debt there is a debt that Philemon
owes to himself, i.e. his *very self*, in the sense that Paul had
brought him to faith in Jesus Christ and to membership of the
Church.

20. *relieve my anxiety*, or 'cheer my heart'. *we are both in Christ*: here, as all through the letter, Paul's bold approach to Philemon is based on the relationship of love that exists between Christians. *in Christ* gives the picture of Jesus as an organism to which Christians belong as its parts. Such a phrase underlines the fact that (*a*) Christians owe all to Jesus and are nothing without him, and (*b*) Christians are tied up together in one fellowship, and so belong to each other.

21-22. Paul is confident that in his treatment of Onesimus Philemon will not be content with the bare minimum that love demands. Paul's request for a *room* or 'hospitality' (another possible translation) shows that he hopes soon to be freed from his imprisonment. This hope can also be seen in Phil. 1: 19, 'Yes, and rejoice I will, knowing well that the issue of it all will be my deliverance.' *in answer to your prayers* shows the importance that Paul attached to intercession or prayer to God for the needs of others. For him this is one of the ways in which we help forward God's purposes and bring help to other people (2 Cor. 1: 11, 'Yes, he will continue to deliver us, if you will co-operate by praying for us'). See also p. 40. ✻

CLOSING GREETINGS

Epaphras, Christ's captive like myself, sends you greet- 23
ings. So do Mark, Aristarchus, Demas, and Luke, my 24
fellow-workers.

The grace of the Lord Jesus Christ be with your spirit! 25

✻ The concluding part of Paul's letters often, as here, contains greetings from various people who are with Paul, e.g. Col. 4: 10-14, where Epaphras, Mark, Aristarchus, Demas and Luke are mentioned, as in the present passage. The conclusion of an ancient letter was usually in the form 'fare you well', an expression of good wishes. Paul substitutes a reference to the 'grace of the Lord Jesus Christ'. See also above on Col. 4: 18.

23. *Epaphras* had had an important part in the founding of the church at Colossae (Col. 1: 7-8). He came from Colossae, and is obviously much trusted by Paul. See also p. 130. *Christ's captive* almost certainly means that Epaphras is also in prison, but we do not know any details. The phrase can be compared with verse 1, where Paul describes himself as 'a prisoner of Christ Jesus'.

24. *Mark* is almost certainly the 'John Mark' of Acts 12: 12; it was at the house of his mother that the Christians met in the early days of the Church in Jerusalem. For his desertion of Paul and Barnabas on their important journey into Asia Minor, see Acts 13: 5 and 13. His action led later to a quarrel between Barnabas, his cousin, and Paul (Acts 15: 37-39). He is now, however, restored to Paul's confidence. By tradition he is the writer of our second Gospel. For further details about Mark see p. 163.

Aristarchus came from Thessalonica, and had probably been known to Paul since the founding of the church there (Acts 17: 1-9). He was one of the representatives of the churches who were accompanying Paul on his journey to Jerusalem (Acts 20: 4). He was also with Paul on the journey to Rome (Acts 27: 2) and was probably one of the 'other prisoners' mentioned in Acts 27: 1. Hence in Col. 4: 10 he is called 'Christ's captive like myself'. See also p. 163.

Demas is mentioned also in Col. 4: 14. From 2 Tim. 4: 10 it seems that later he deserted Paul, 'because his heart was set on this world'.

Luke is further described in Col. 4: 14 as 'our dear friend Luke, the doctor'. His loyalty is also referred to in 2 Tim. 4: 11 ('I have no one with me but Luke'). He may have been using his medical skill in caring for Paul's health during his imprisonment. By tradition he is the author of the two-volume work, the Gospel of Luke and the Acts of the Apostles. See further on p. 165.

25. Philippians ends in a similar way. The concluding greeting in Paul's letters, like the opening, always includes the word *grace*. The best of 'good wishes' that Paul can convey to those addressed is that they may enjoy all the benefits of God's love and favour brought to us in Jesus. *your spirit* is the same as 'you'. ✶

✶ ✶ ✶ ✶ ✶ ✶ ✶ ✶ ✶ ✶ ✶ ✶ ✶

WHY SHOULD WE VALUE THIS LETTER TODAY?

(1) *Small things matter*

As we have seen, Philemon differs from Paul's other surviving letters in that it approximates more closely to the private note. On the surface the subject of the letter is very trivial. The question of a 'runaway slave' may seem very small compared with the big issues discussed in Paul's other letters, e.g. the problems of church discipline in 1 Corinthians, the highlights of Christian doctrine in Ephesians and Colossians. There may be a sense of a drop from a height. But this contrast points the moral that for the Christian no one or no thing is too trivial for deep concern. Paul himself gives the same attention and seriousness to the present problem as he would to major issues striking at the life of the Church. In this Paul is acting on the teaching of Jesus: 'If anyone wants to be first, he must make himself last of all and servant of all' (Mark 9: 35). Paul must have had plenty on his mind to occupy him, but nevertheless he 'had time' for a runaway slave, whom some might have dismissed 'as useless rubbish'. One of the great characteristics, however, of Christian love is that it has time for people whoever they are and whatever kind of people they are.

(2) *The best advice*

Paul's method of approach to Philemon is also instructive. As one with the authority of an apostle, he could have laid down a course of action for Philemon, and told him what his duty was. He prefers to treat Philemon as a responsible being on whose love he can rely. It is so easy in giving advice to other people to 'lay down the law' and make them feel as though they have no minds of their own. Often the starting-point for helping others is to treat them as real people who can be trusted. All through the letter Paul is sure that he can rely upon Philemon to do the right thing. He will not force a decision on his friend; he will make an appeal in an atmosphere of confidence, and show the difference that Christianity makes to the 'master–slave' relationship. It is then for Philemon to make up his mind for himself. This points to the important fact that the big thing in giving advice is not to 'dictate', but to help the other person to clarify his mind and see the issues involved and so come to a decision.

✻ ✻ ✻ ✻ ✻ ✻ ✻ ✻ ✻ ✻ ✻ ✻ ✻

INDEX

Abba, 'Father', Jesus' way of addressing God, 32
access, approach to God, 51, 57
Achaia, a Roman province, x, 83, 156
Acts of the Apostles, 16, 113, 130, 165, 190; also quoted in many places
Adam, the type of the man who is disobedient to God, 73, 152
adoption as sons of God, 33
advent of Jesus, his coming to reign, 13, 76, 91, 140, 150
afflictions, of Christ, 139
age, the present, 42
age to come, 42, 46
Alexander the Great, 117
ambassador, as description of an Apostle, 95, 185
angels, 58, 105, 120, 135
anger, 75, 152
animal sacrifice, 77
Antigonus of Macedonia, 117
Antioch, ix, 55, 164
Aphrodite, a goddess, 118
apocalyptic writings, 4
Apostle, office of, 29, 129, 182
Apostles, 51, 54
appeal, 180, 185, 192
Apphia, the wife of Philemon of Colossae, 173, 183
arbiter, an umpire, 154
Archippus, 166, 173
Aristarchus, 163, 190
arrows, descriptive of attack by evil forces, 94
Artemas, 18, 162
Asia, a Roman province, ix, x, 1, 18, 113
Athens, x, 20, 70
Athene, a goddess, 118
Augustus, the first Roman Emperor, 31 B.C–A.D 14, 20
authority, an evil power, 94, 135, 144

authorship
  different senses of, 5
  of Colossians, problems of, 104
  of Ephesians, problems of, 6

baptism, 26, 62, 72, 80, 85, 124, 145, 152
barbarian, 152
belt, 94
blessing, a gift of God, 33
blood, in animal sacrifice, 35
body
  of the Church, 23, 43, 50, 62, 71, 84, 148
  of Jesus, 50 87, 111
bond, a certificate of debt, 146
bridegroom, used of God and Jesus, 88
brother, a fellow-Christian, 96, 127, 162, 165, 183
building, used of the Church, 51
burial, 145

Caesarea, ix, 114, 175
catechism, 82, 156
centurion, 49
character
  Christian, 24, 73, 74, 126, 151–5
  of Jesus, 45, 73, 76, 152
cheerful service of slaves, 90
child, an affectionate name for a Christian, 186
children, 88, 157
chosen, by God, 27, 33, 153
Christ, a title and name of Jesus, 31, 128
Chronicles 1 and 2, an Old Testament writing of about 300 B.C., 43, 72, 91
Church, the society founded by Jesus, 23, 43, 57, 60, 66–71, 84, 85–9, 99, 124, 130, 138, 141, 148, 158; see also body, building, house, temple

193

INDEX